The Artwork of Presedo 6

Illustrations by Daniel Lavagna Presedo

© 2019 by Dramenon Studios
Illustrations copyright 2019 by Daniel Presedo

All rights reserved. Published in the United States by Dramenon Studios.
www.dramenon.com
www.presedo.net

The Artwork of Presedo 6 is © 2019 Dramenon Studios. This is a work of fiction. The art and characters, incidents, and dialogues are products of the author's imagination and are not to be construed as real. Any resemblance to actual events or persons, living or dead, is entirely coincidental. None of the contents may be reprinted, except for purposes of review, without the written permissiotn of Dramenon Studios. www.dramenon.com

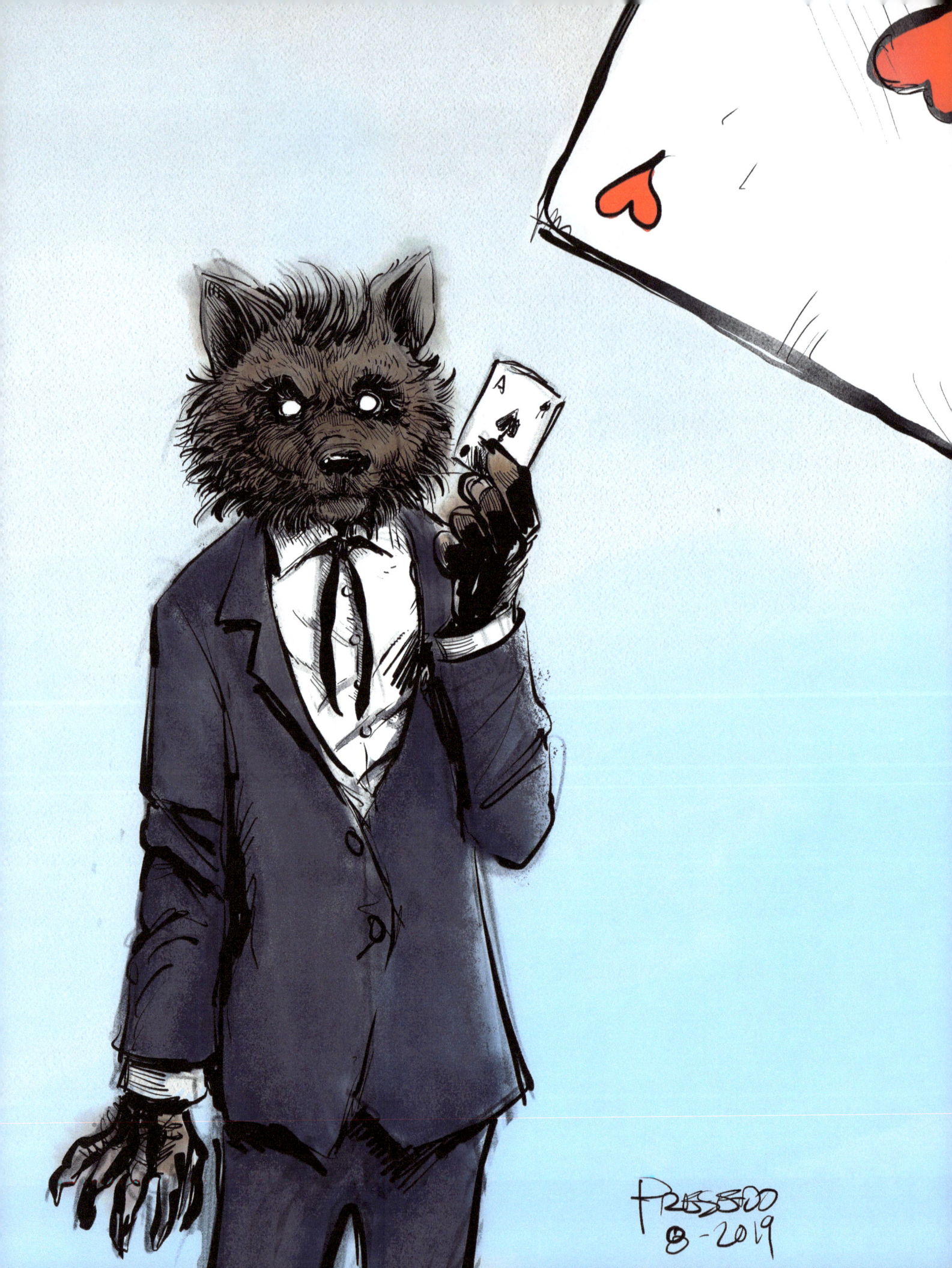

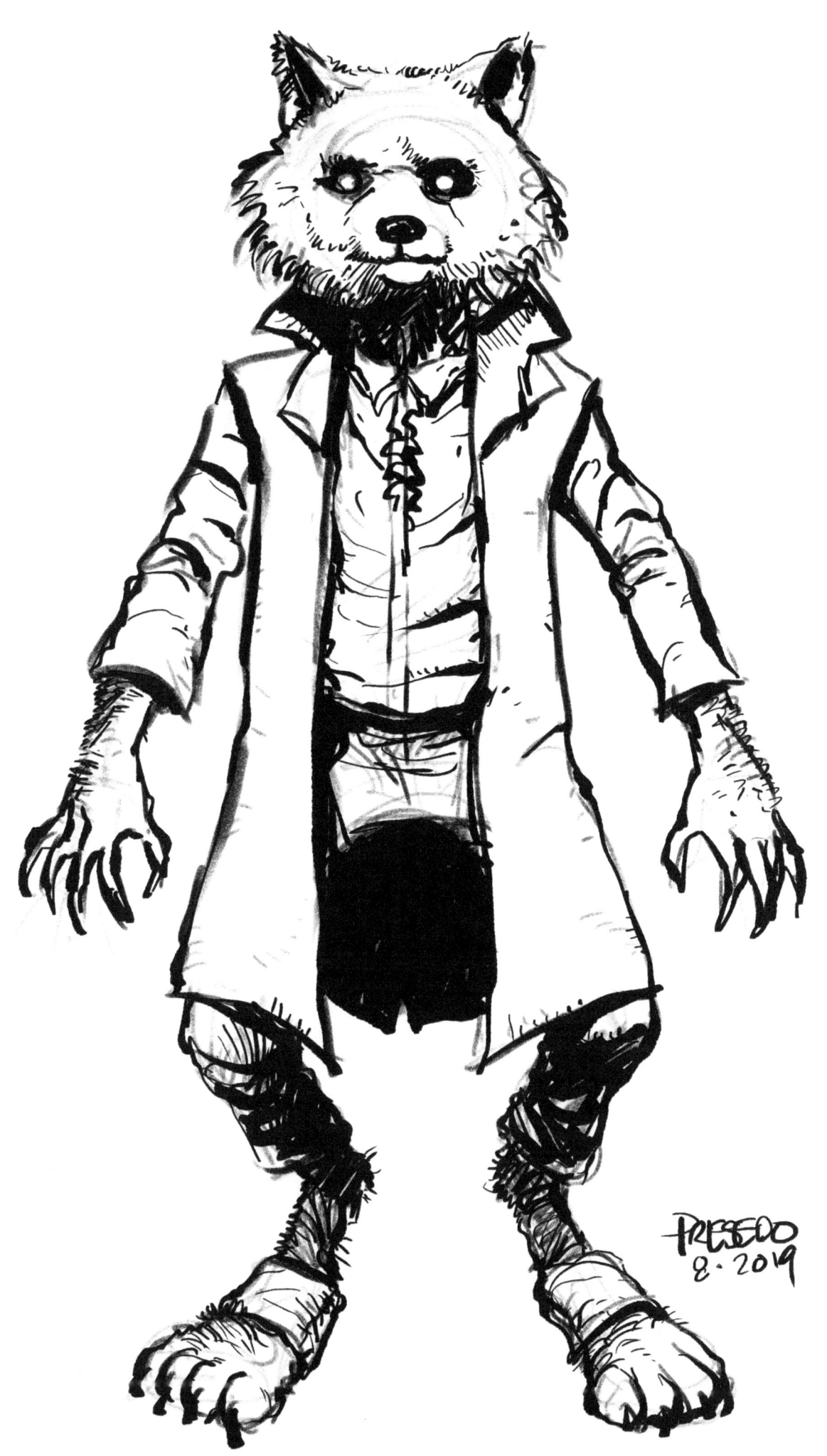

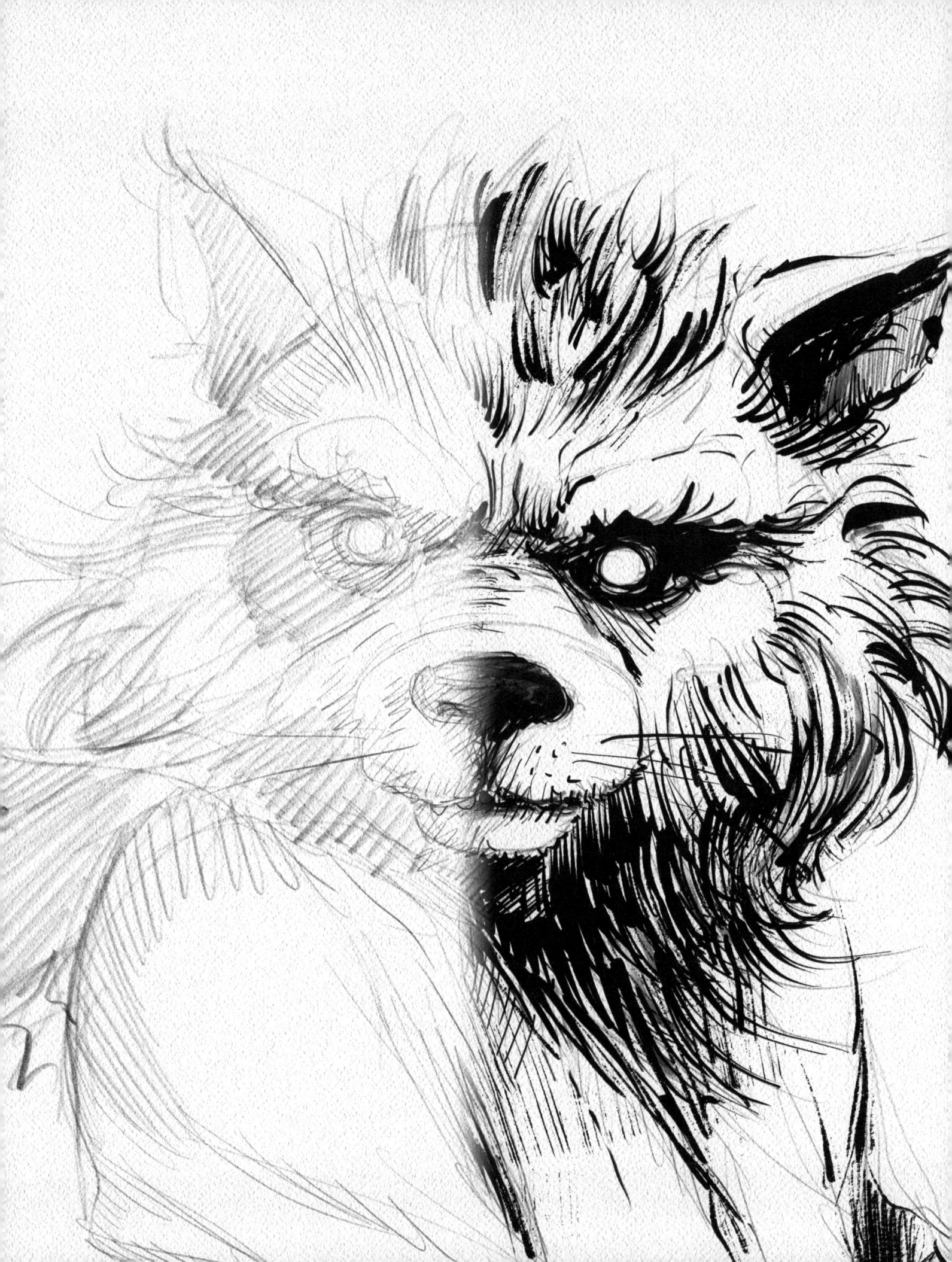

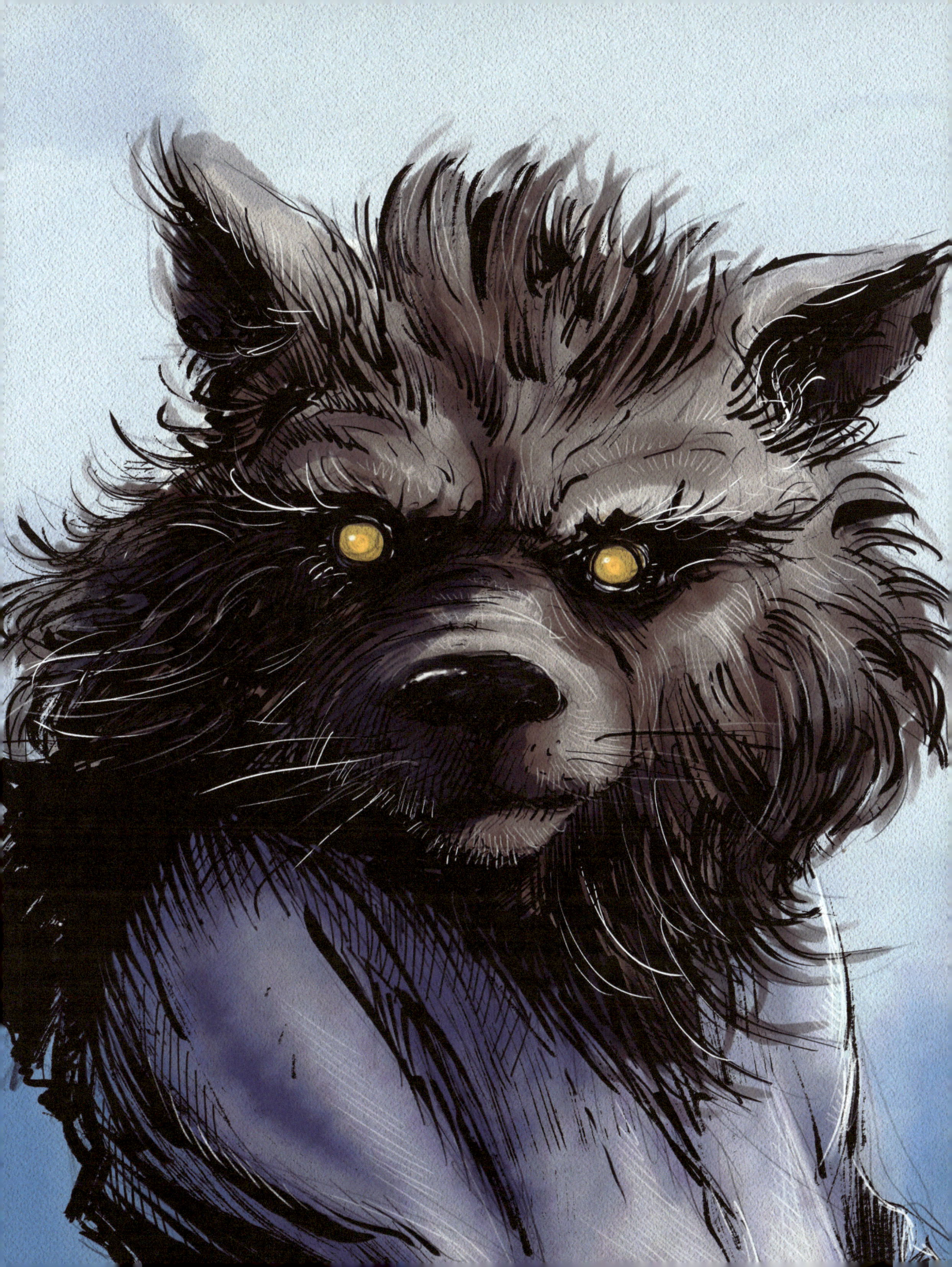

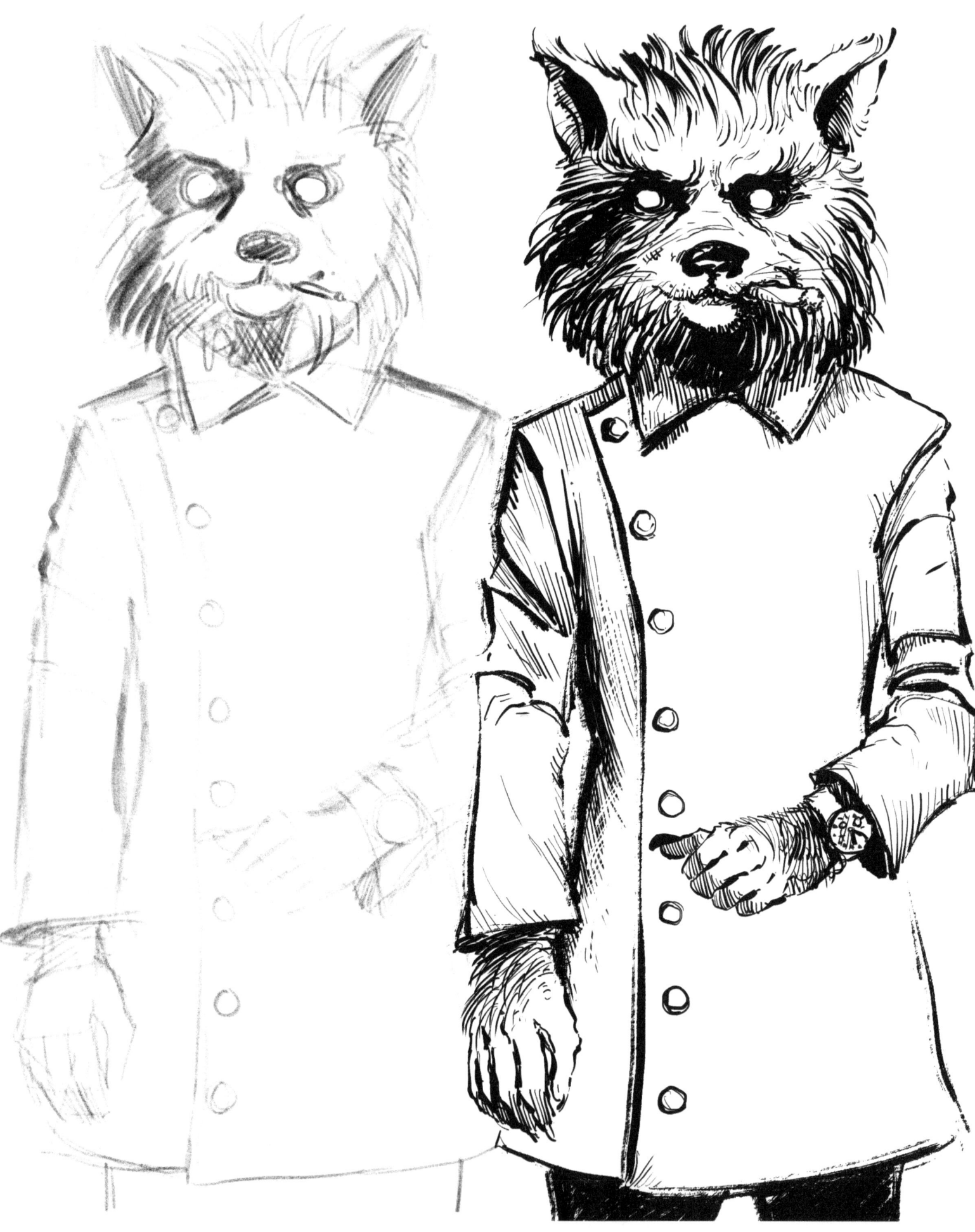

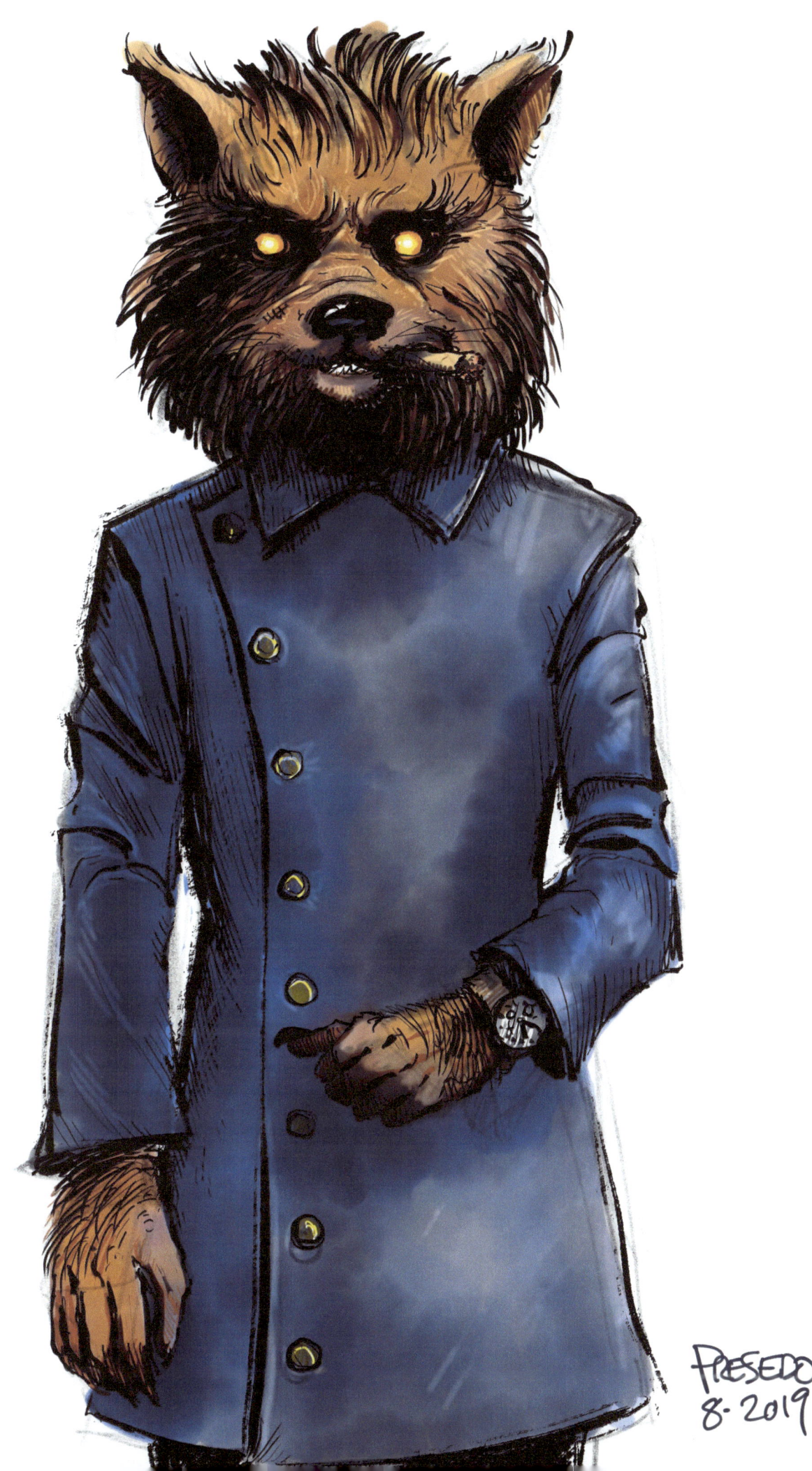

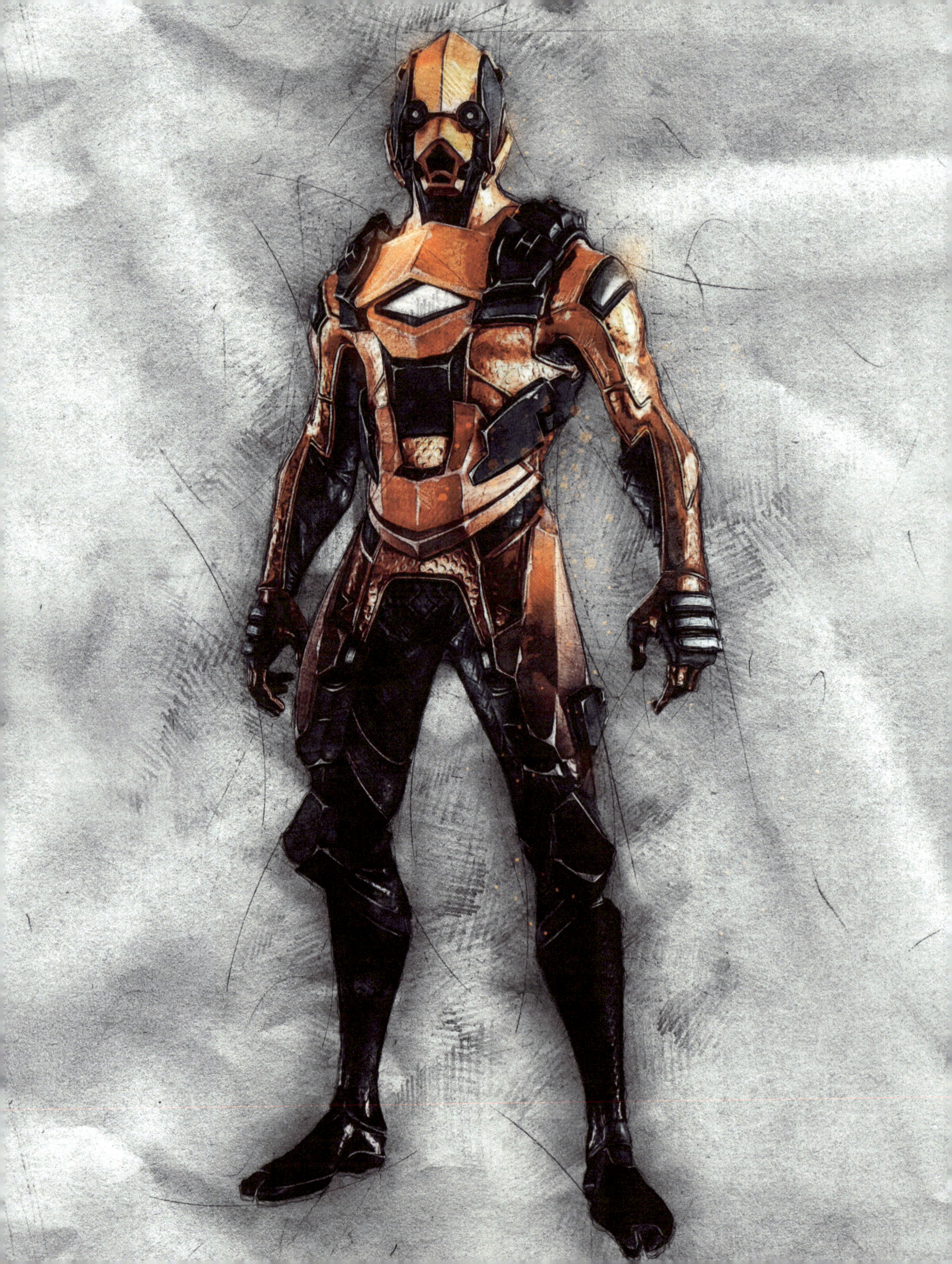

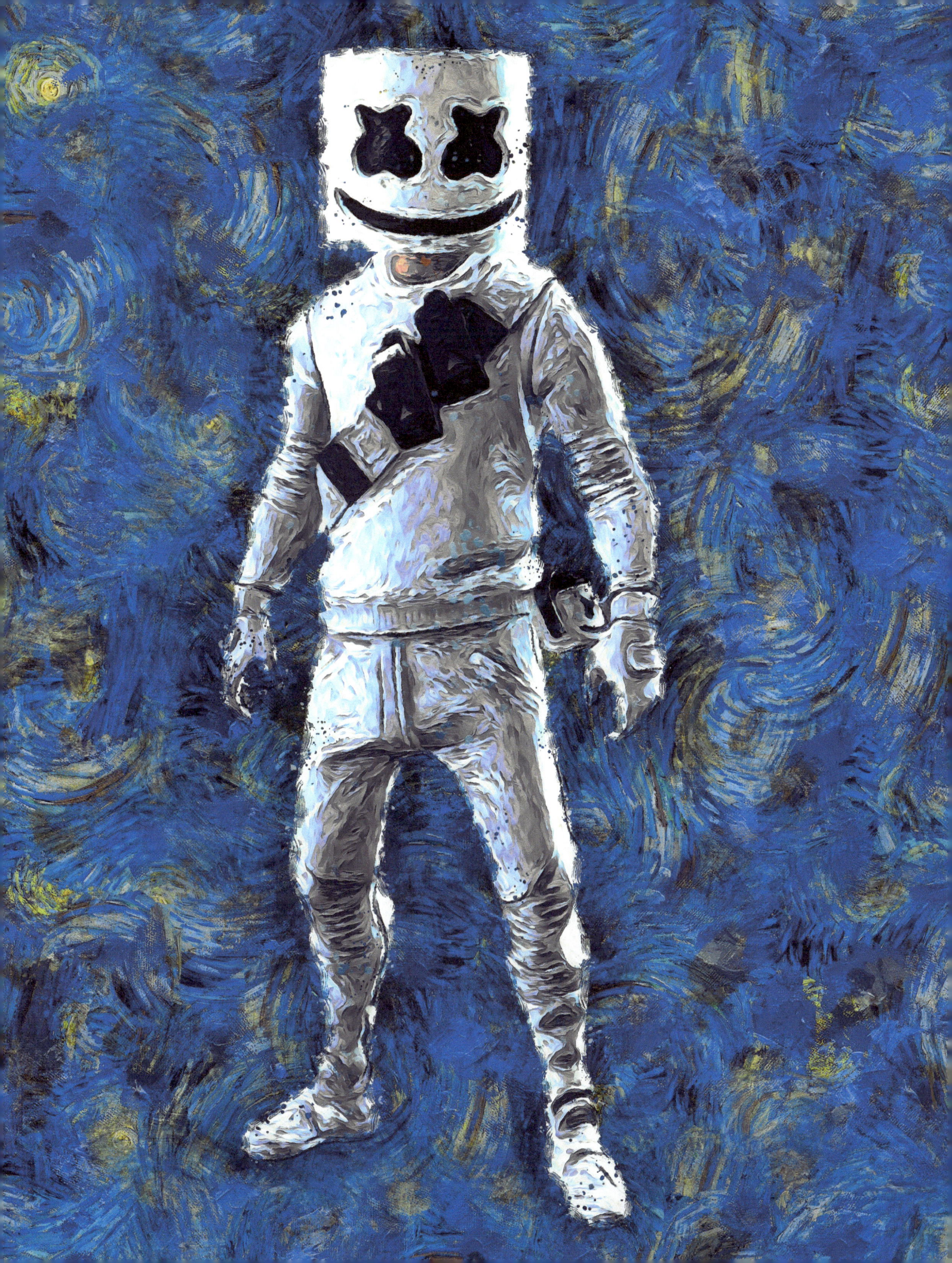

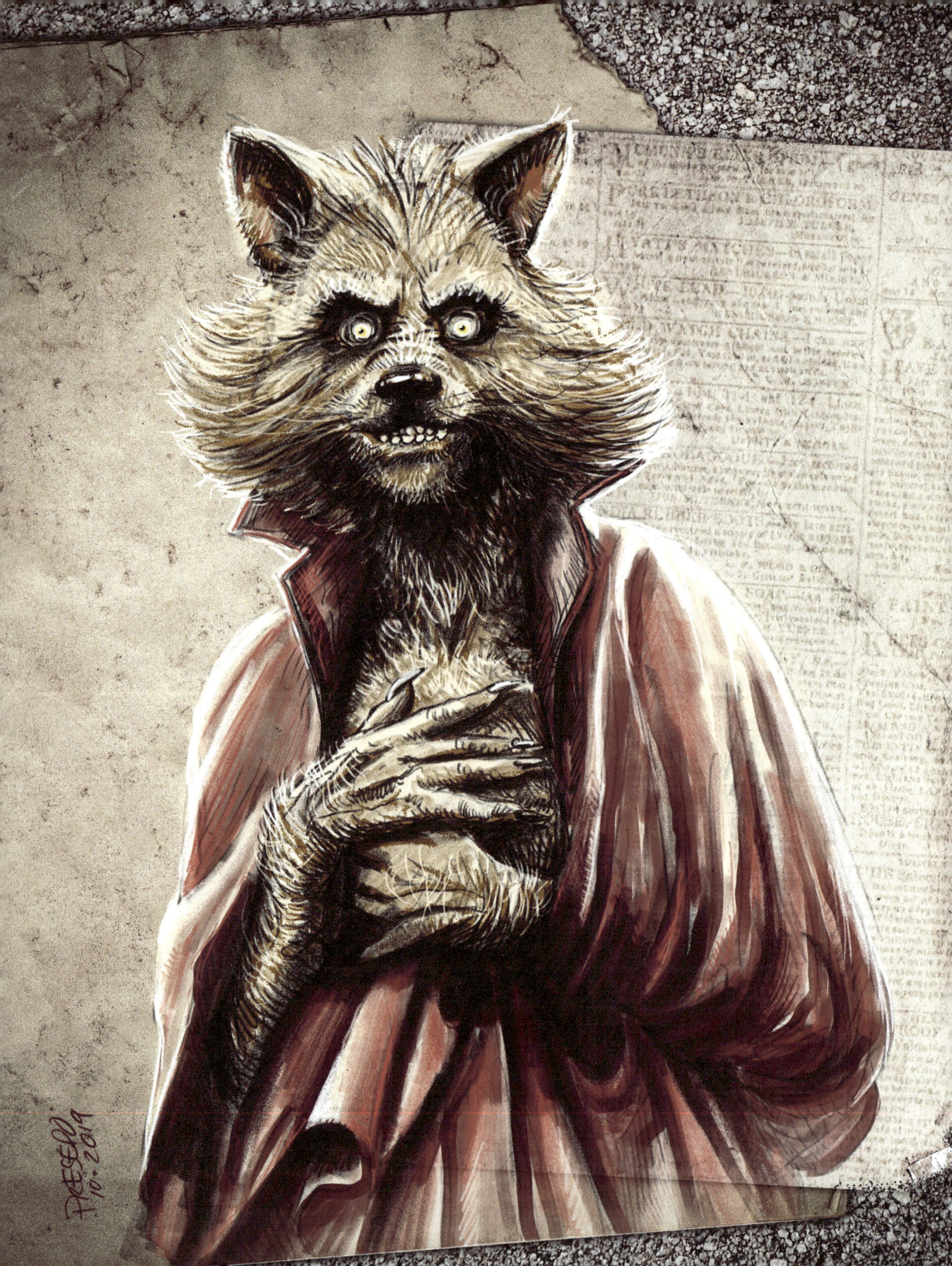

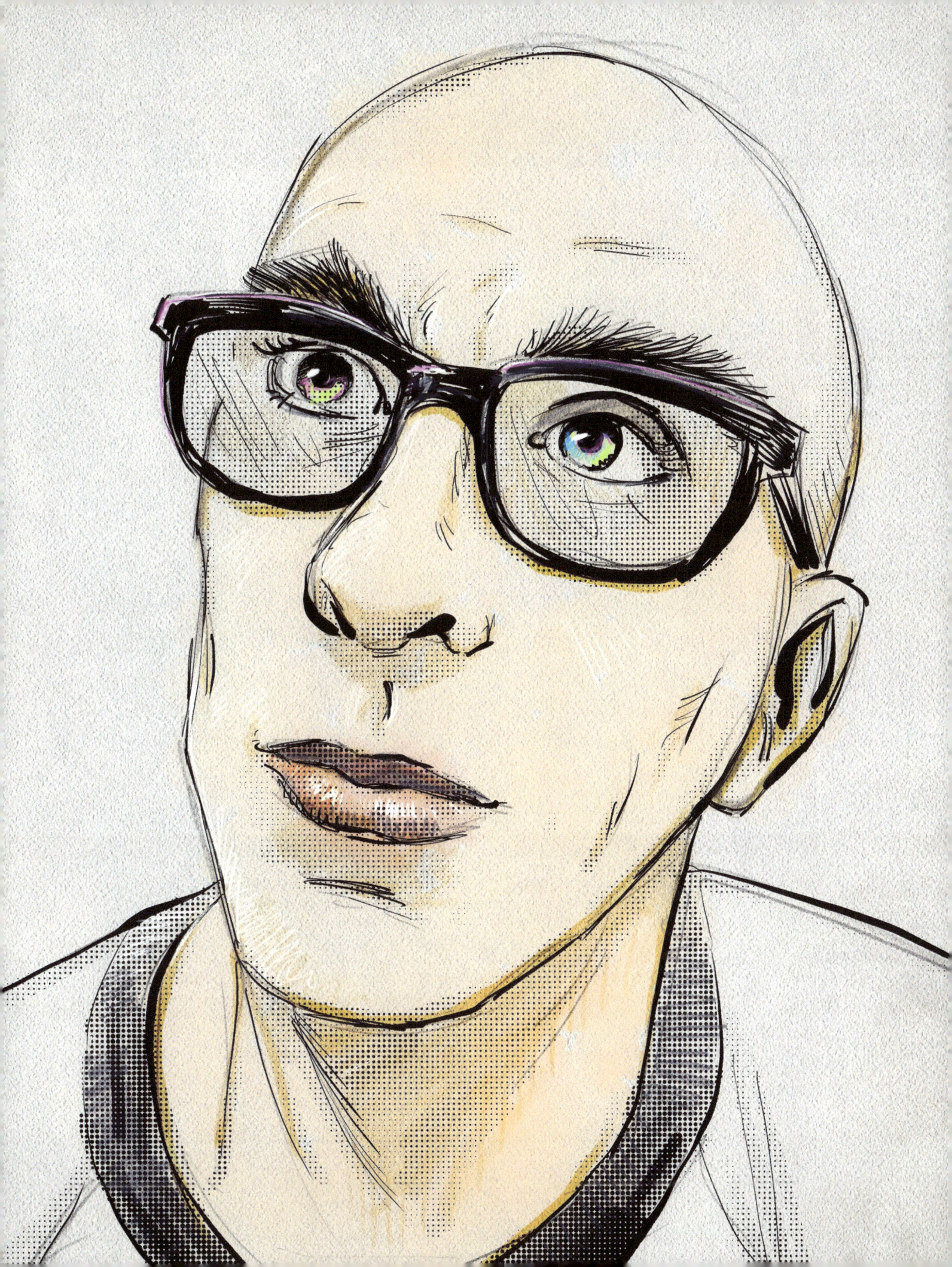

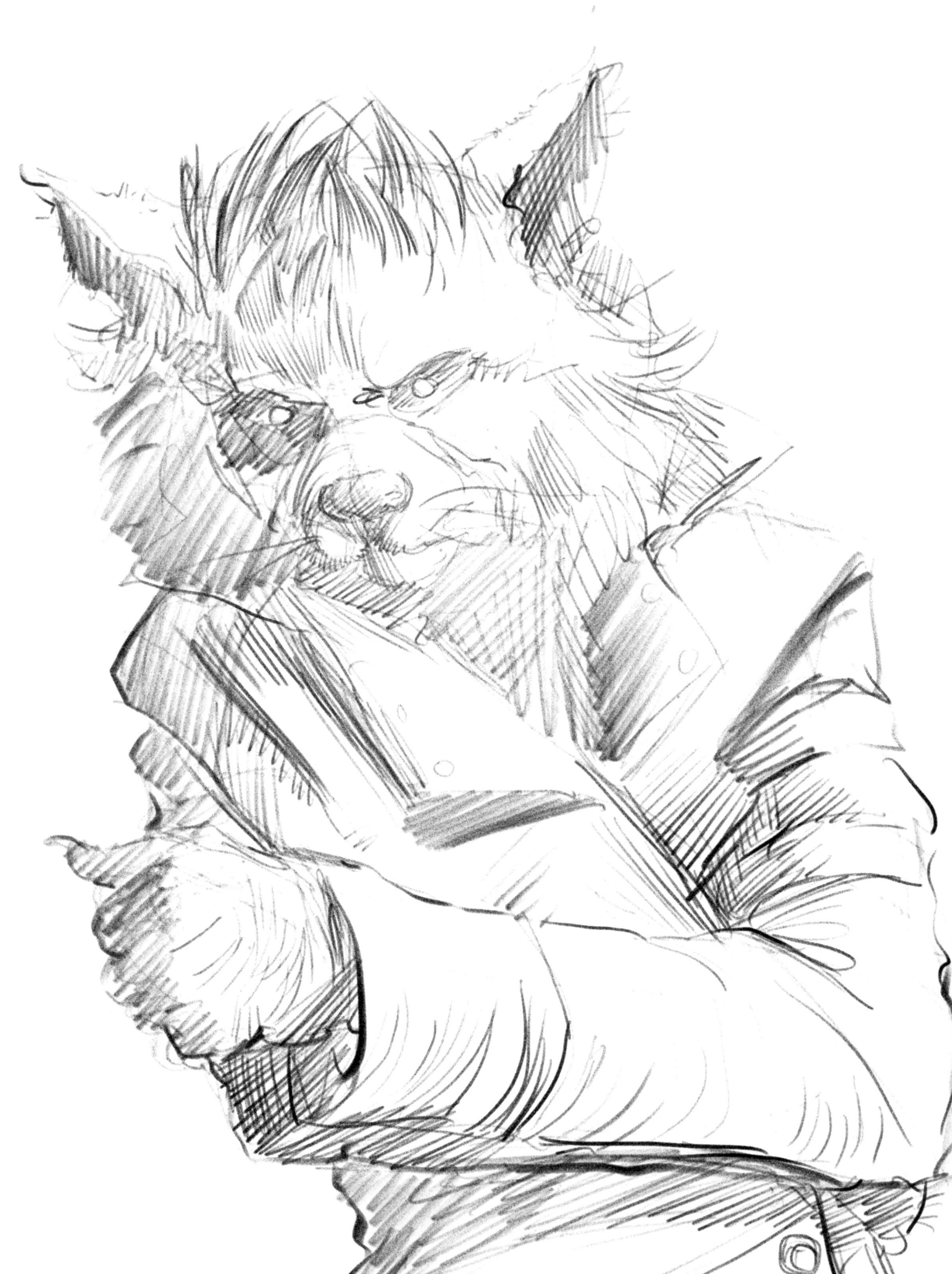

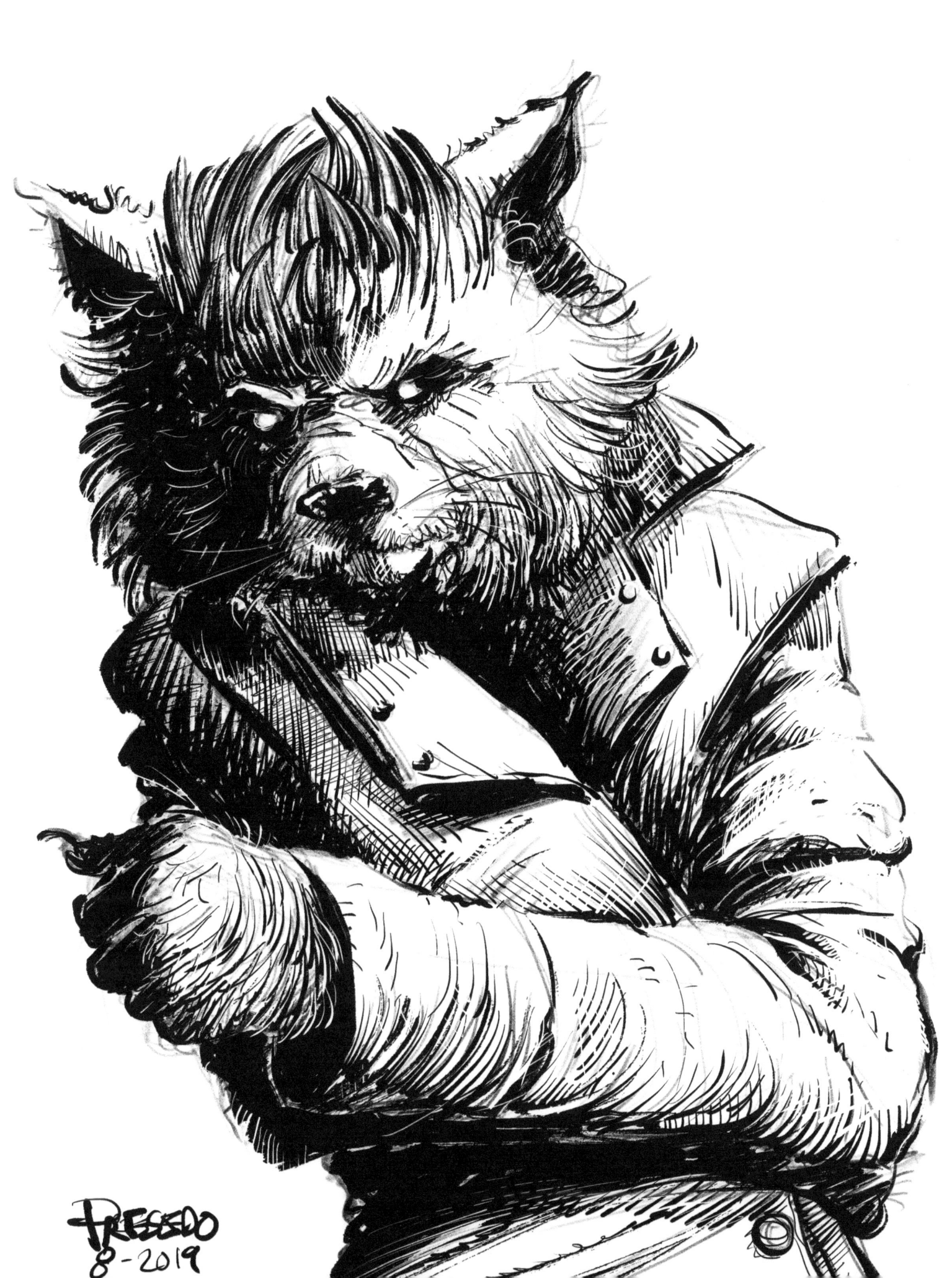

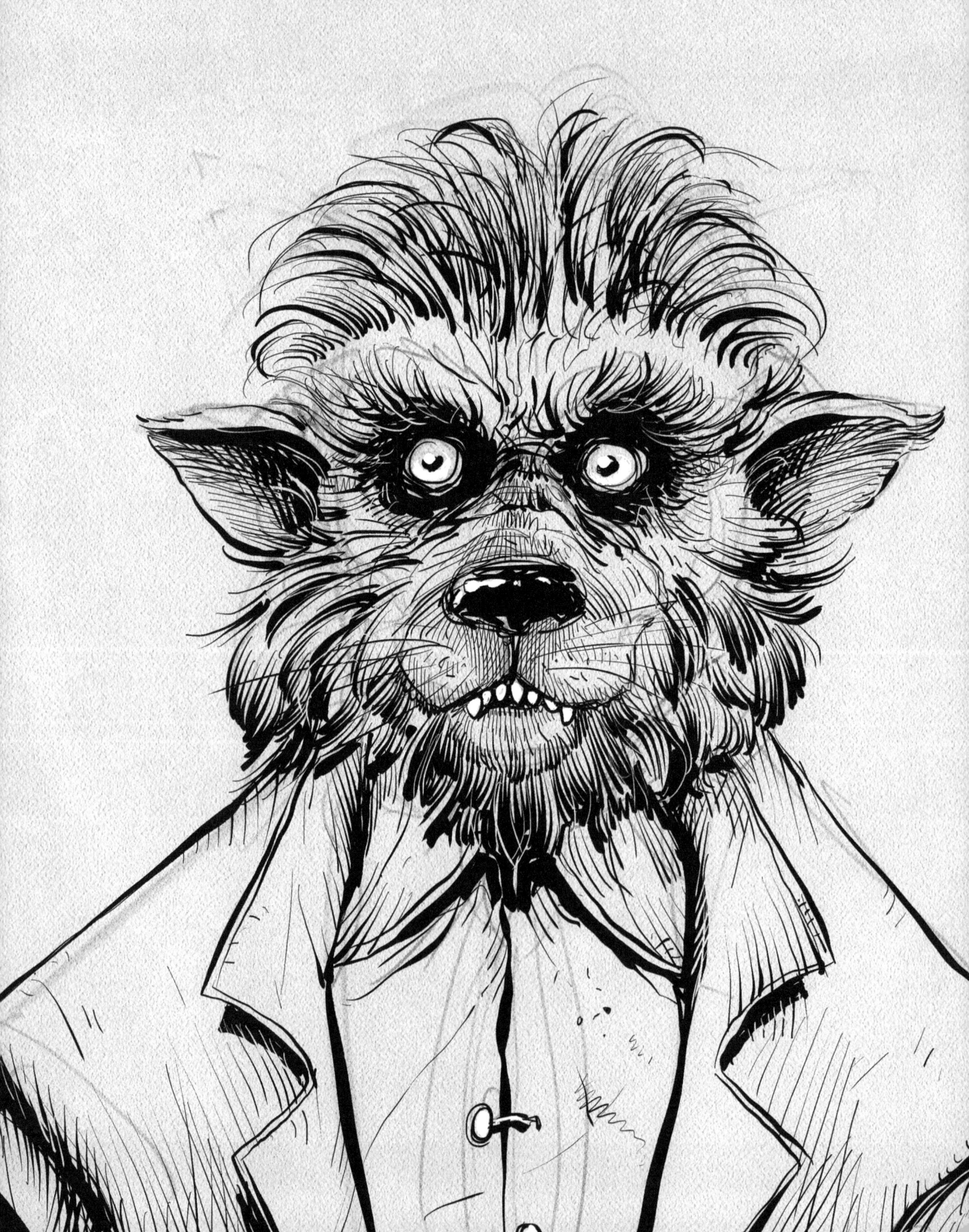

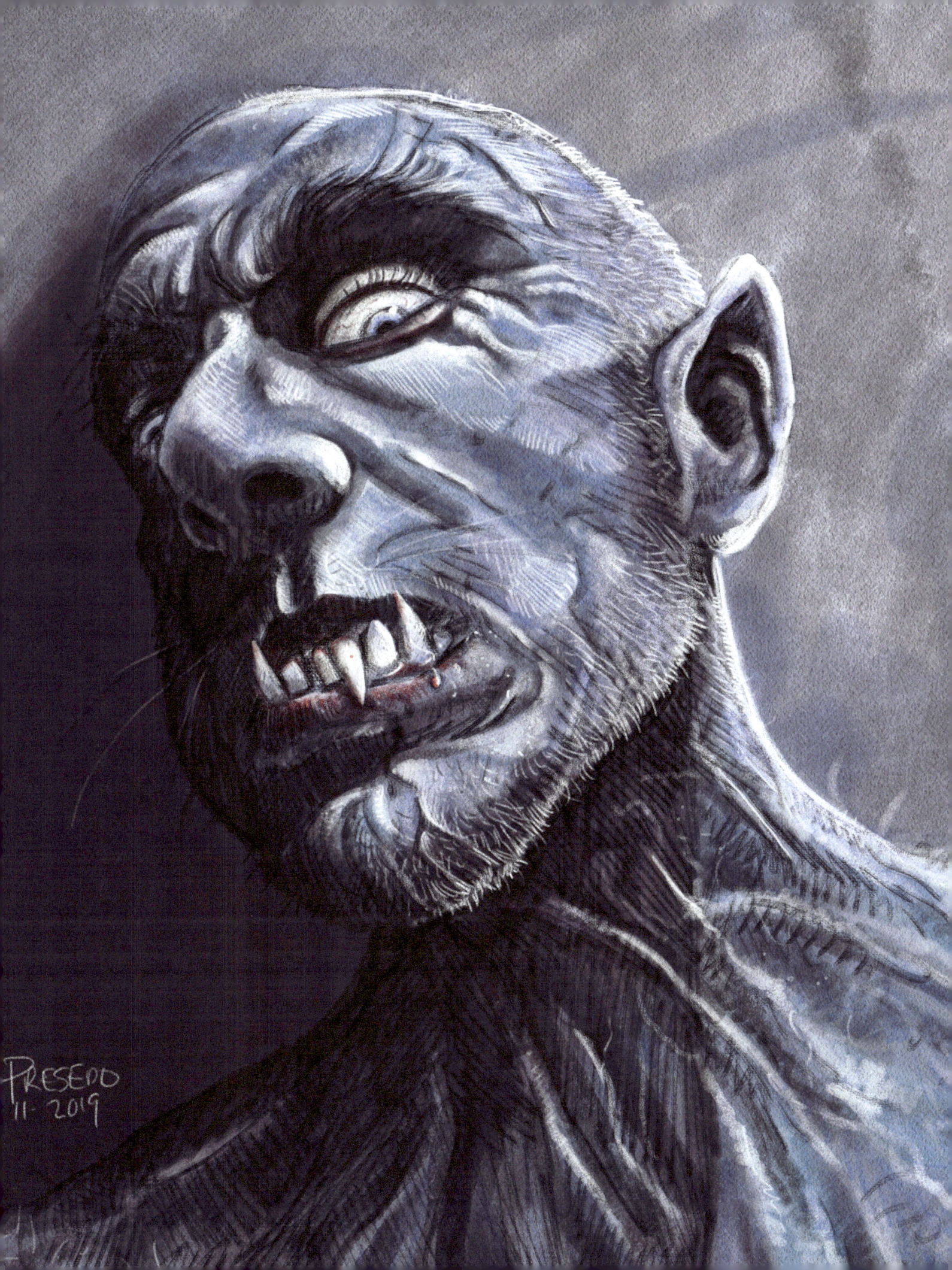

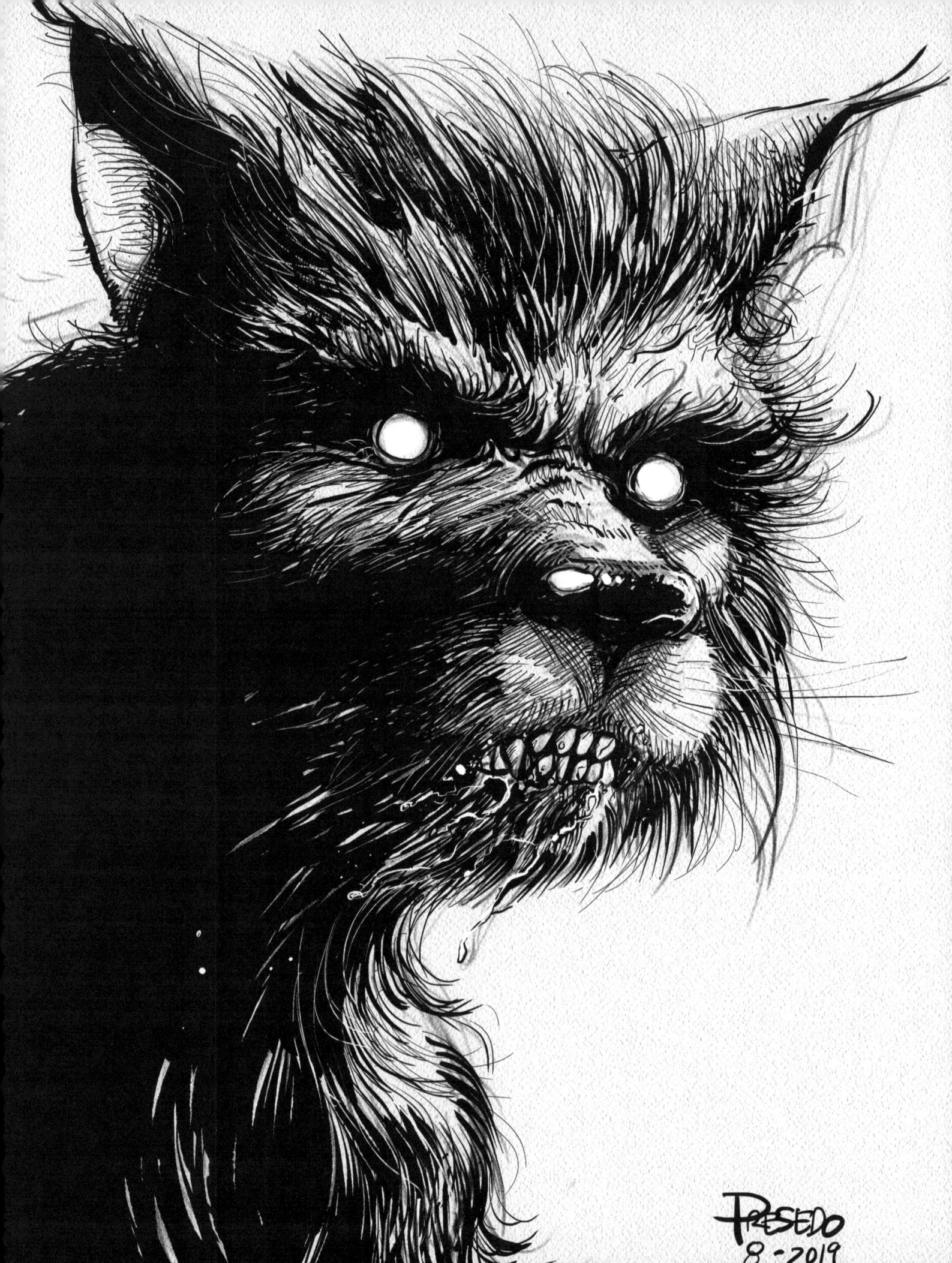

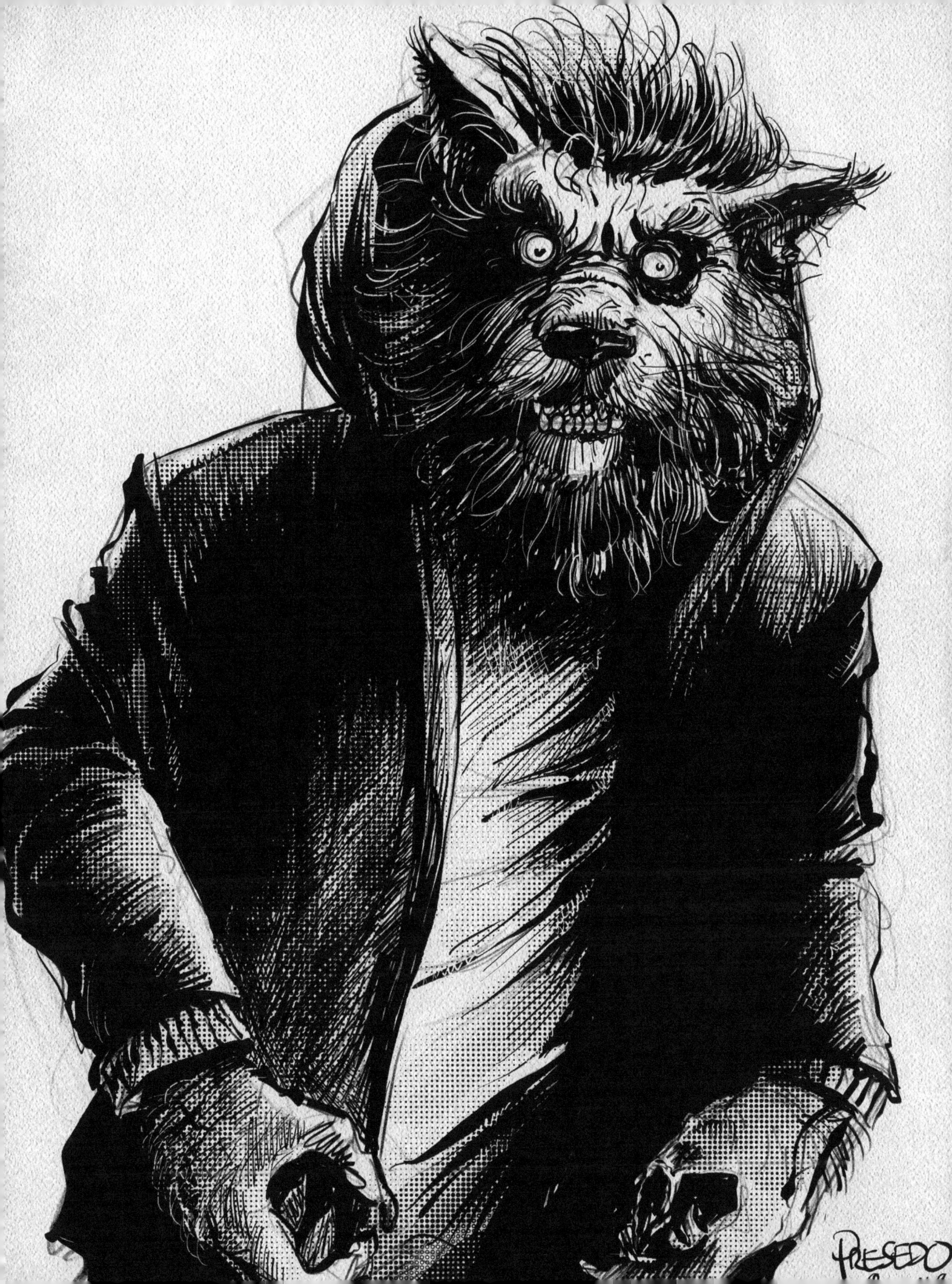

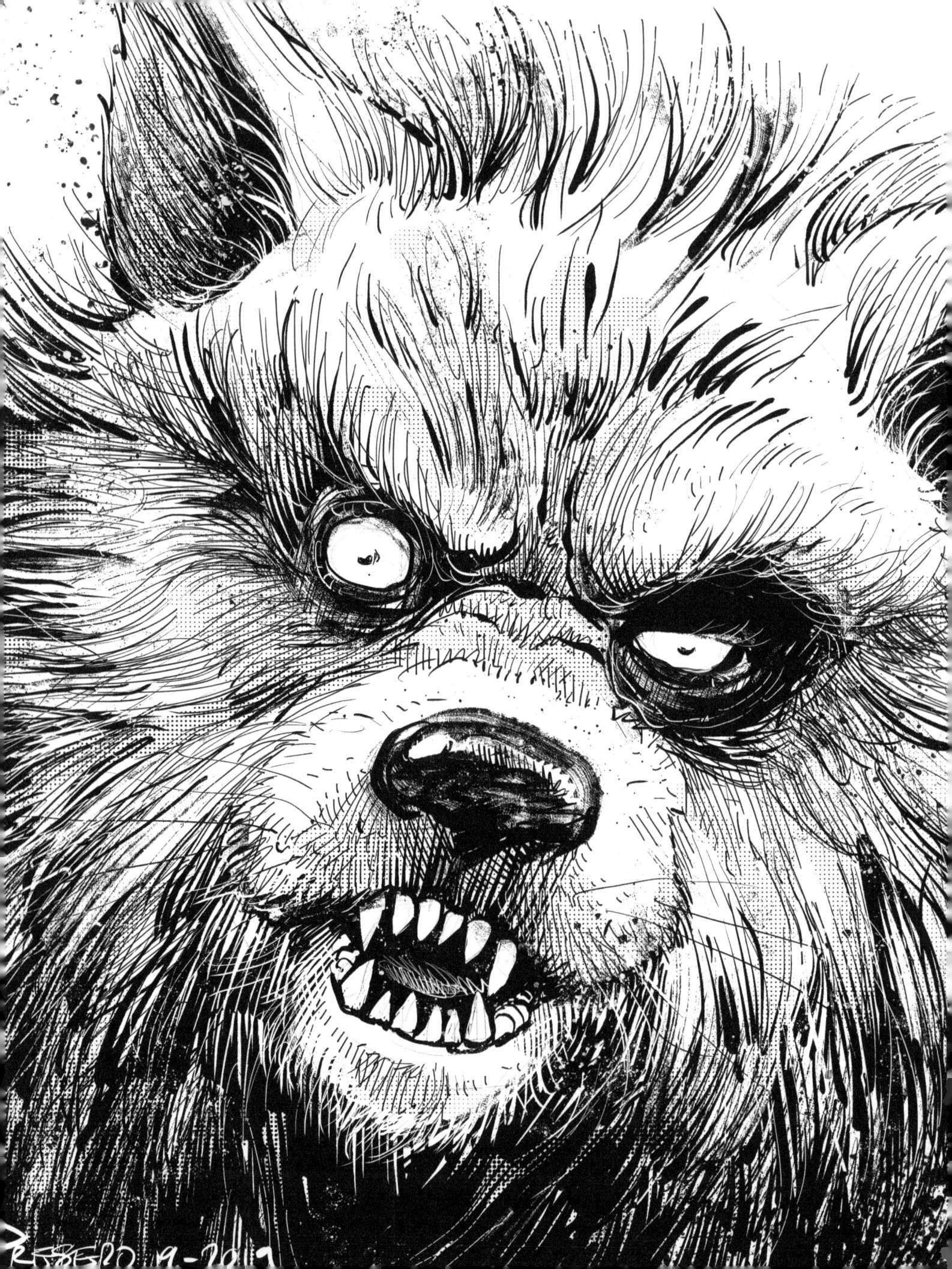

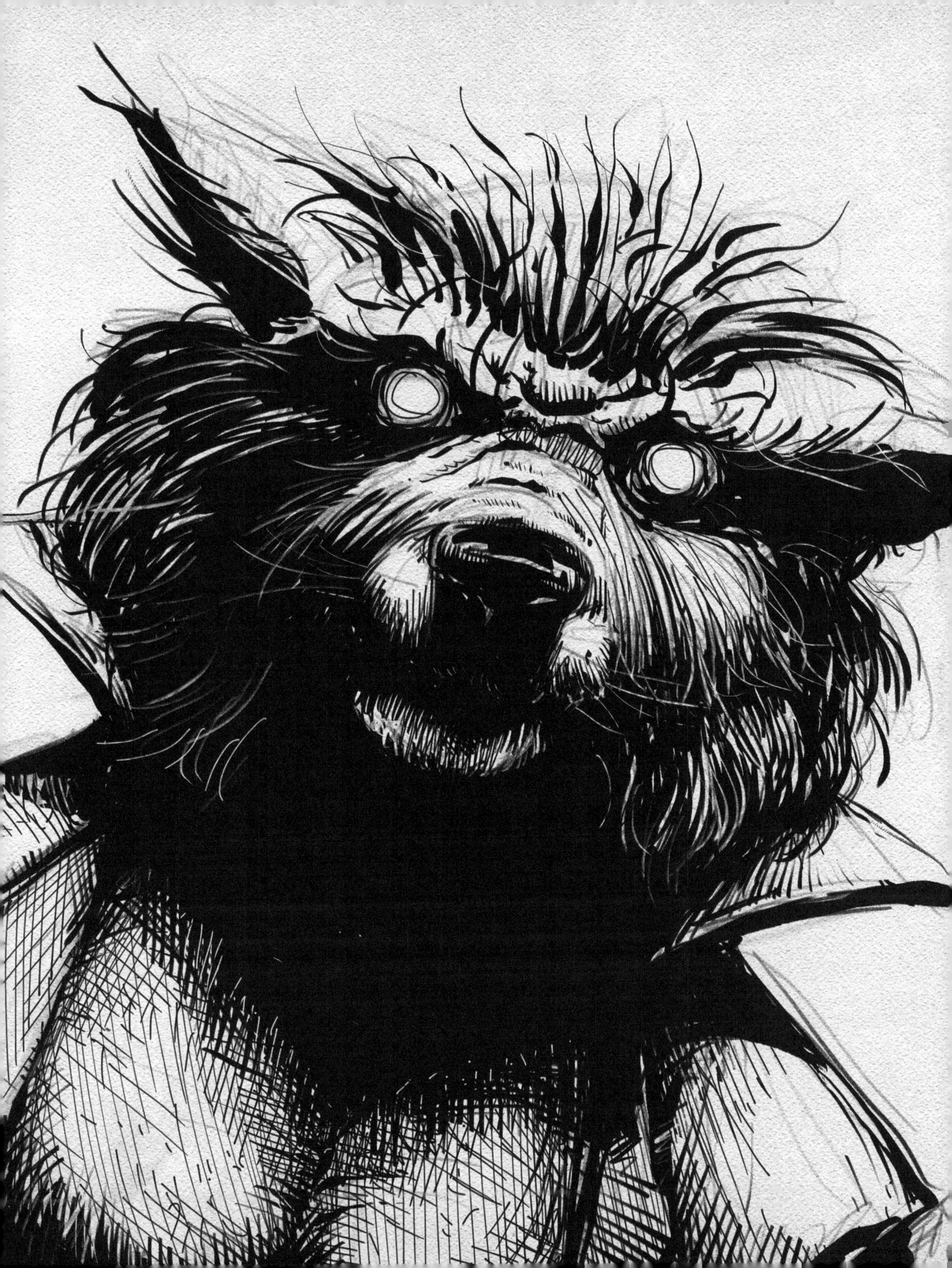

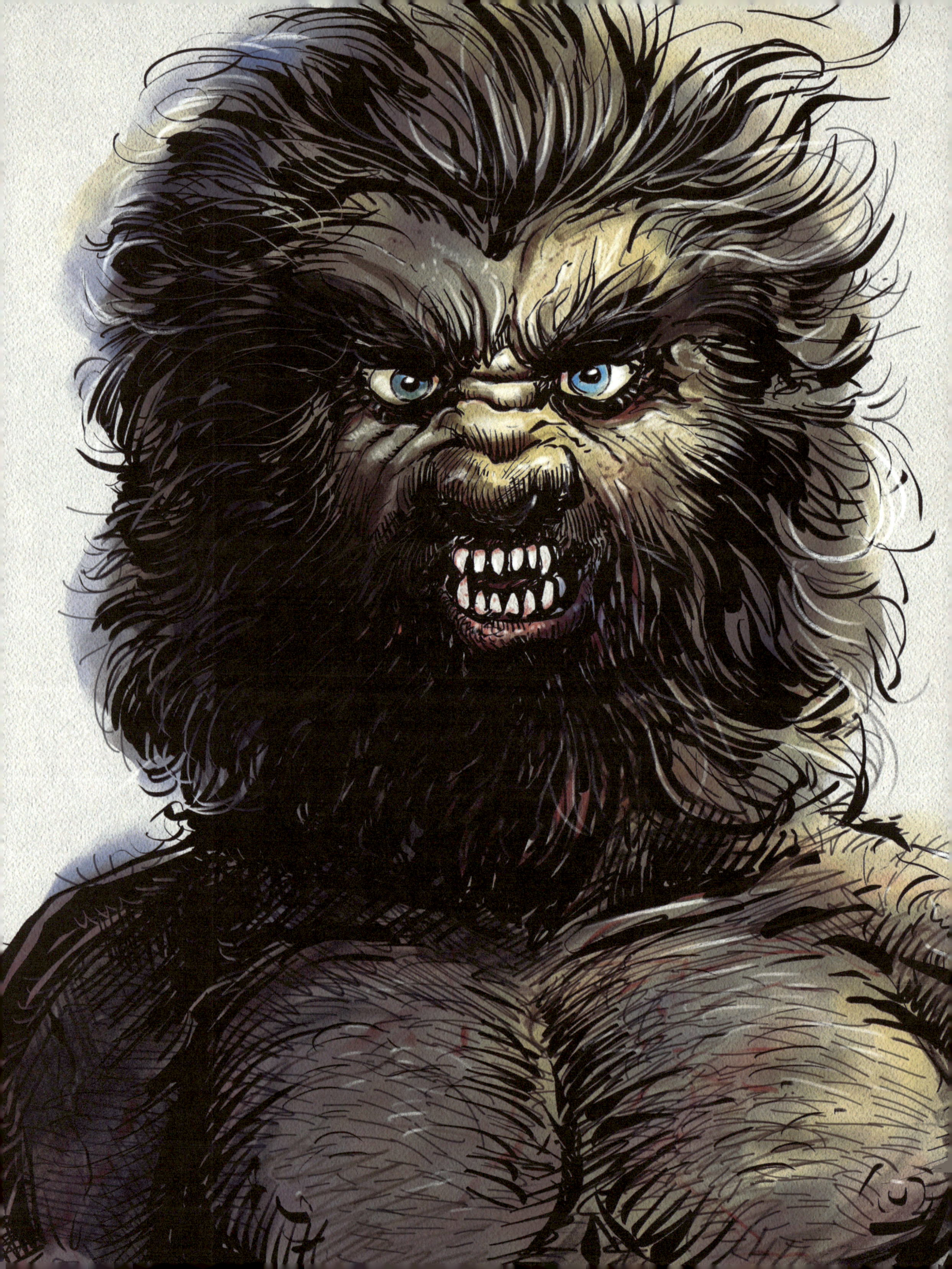

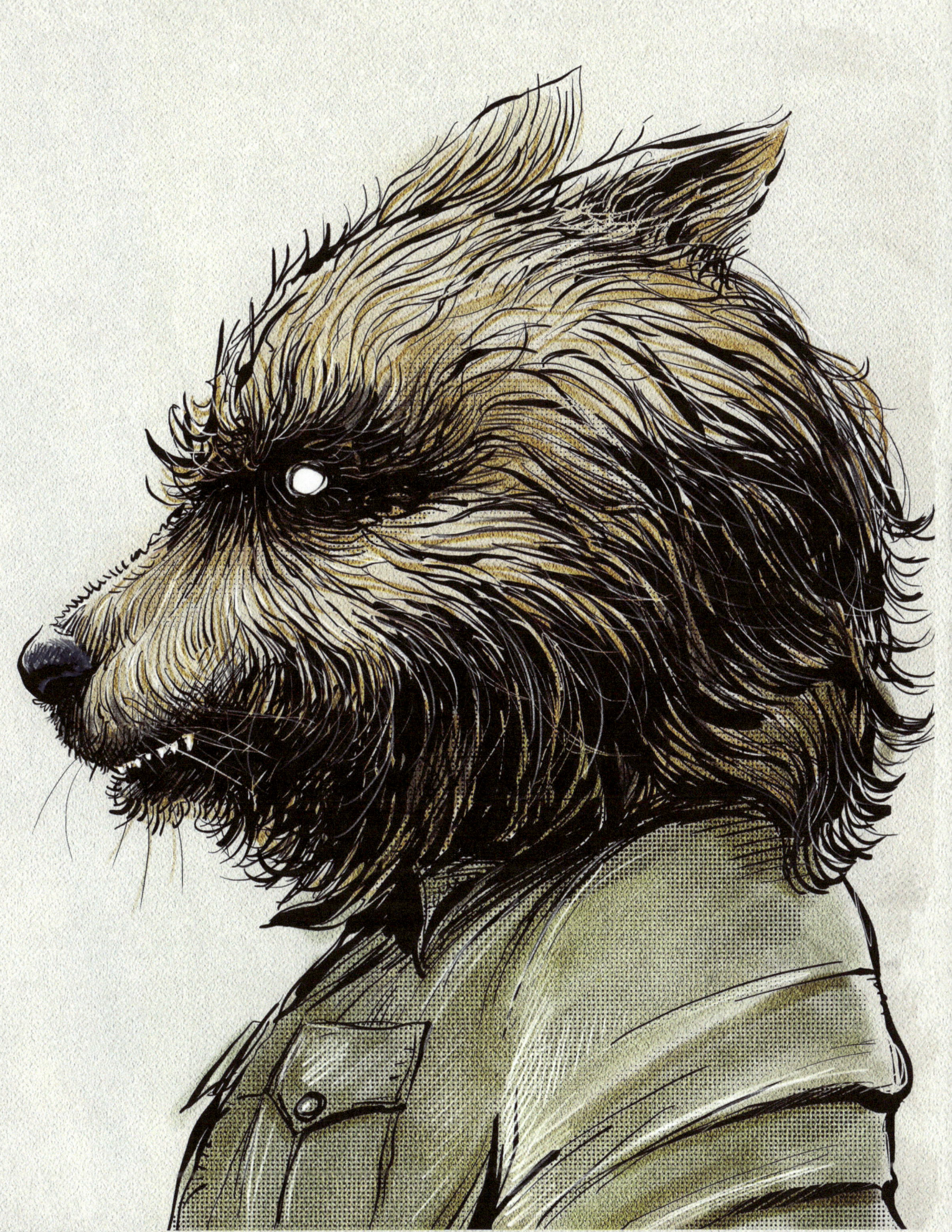

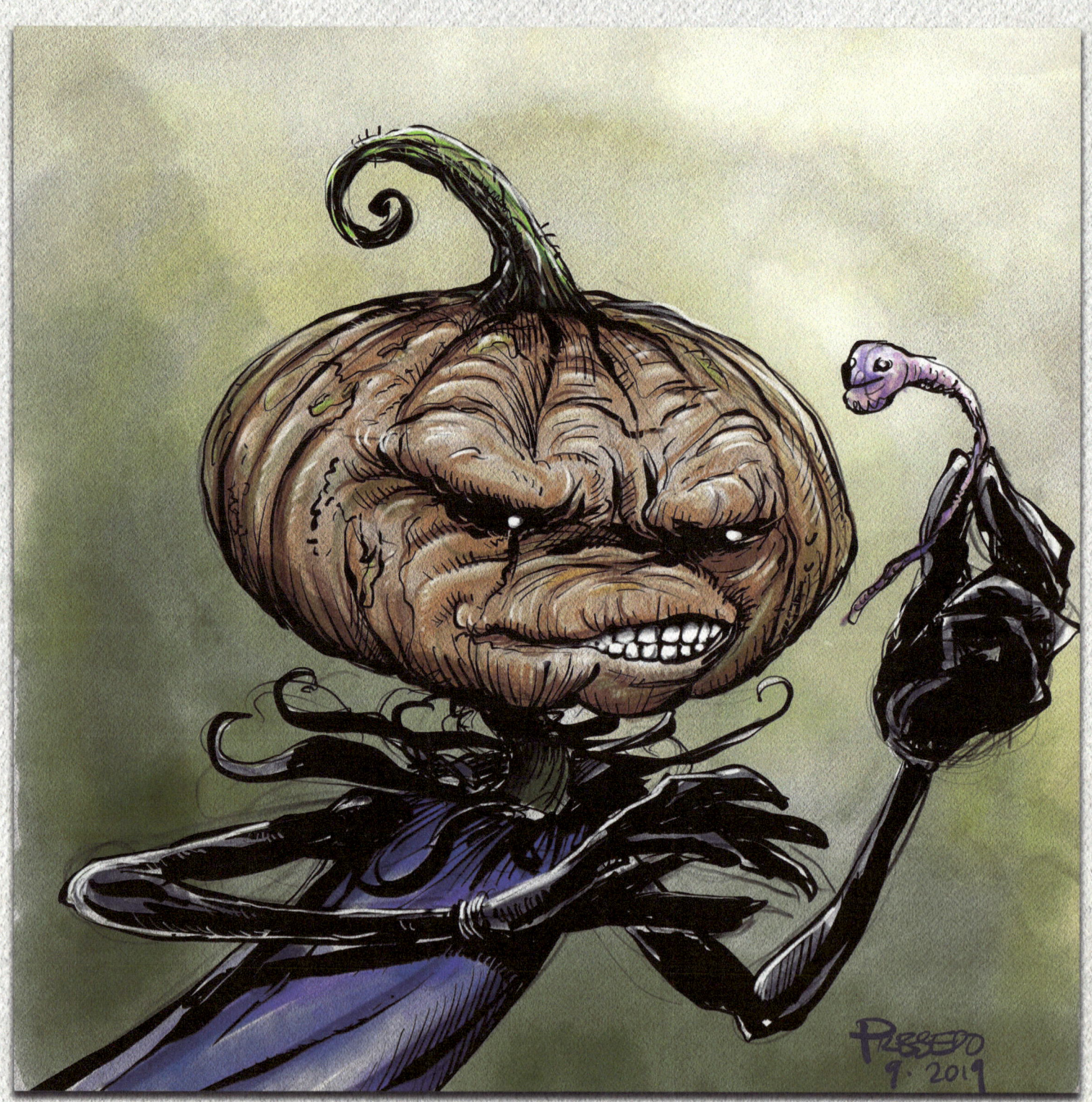

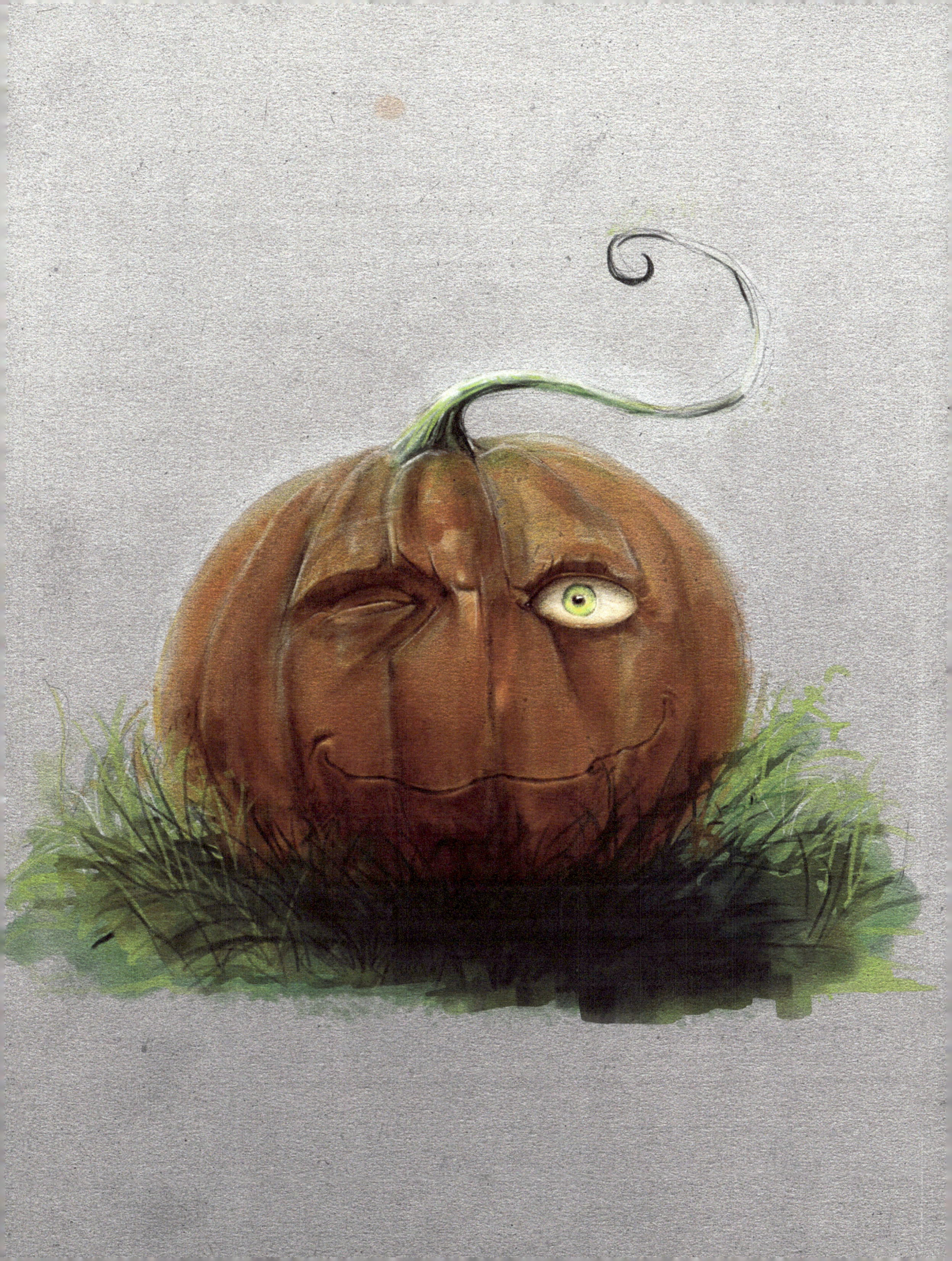

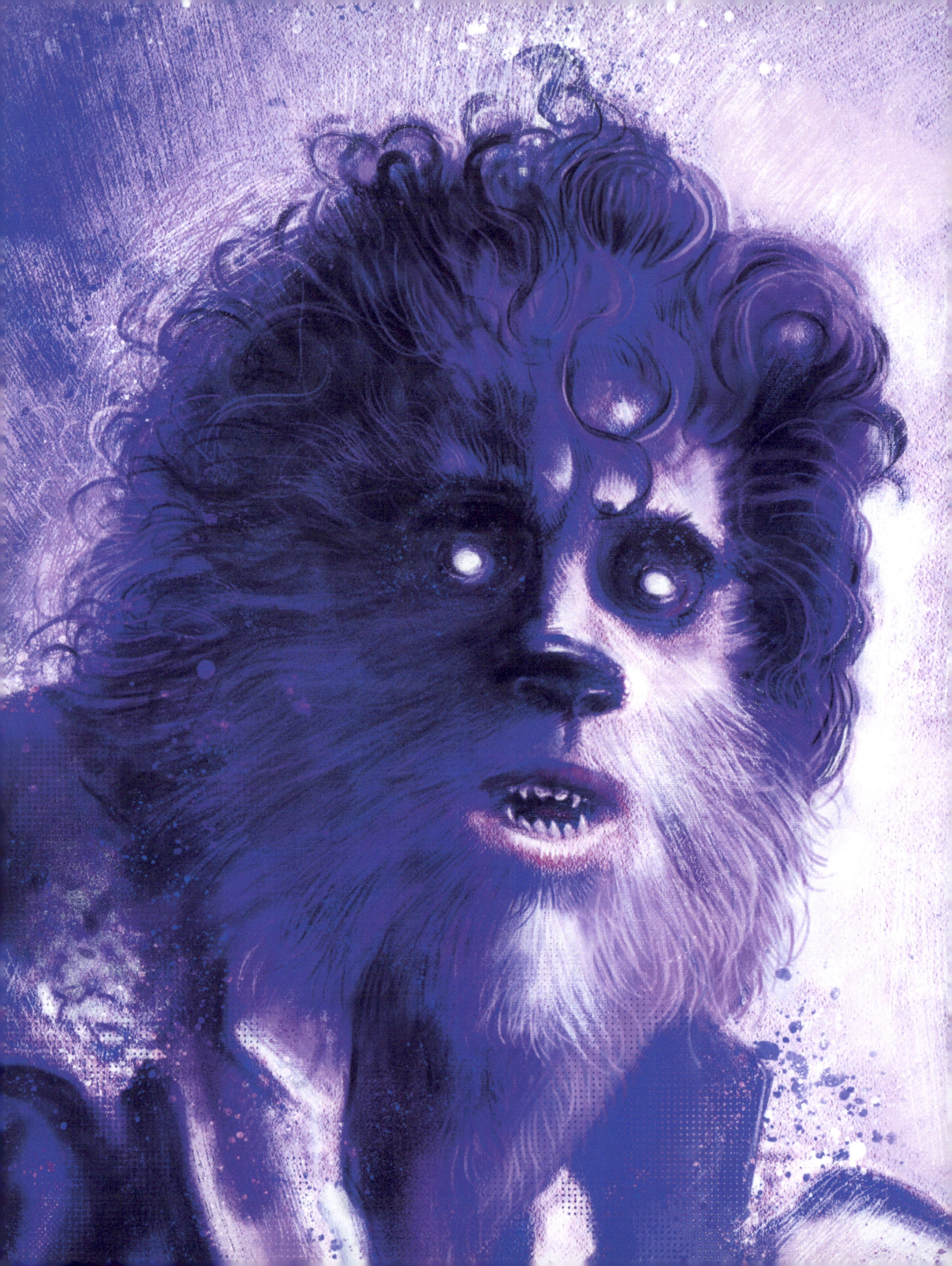

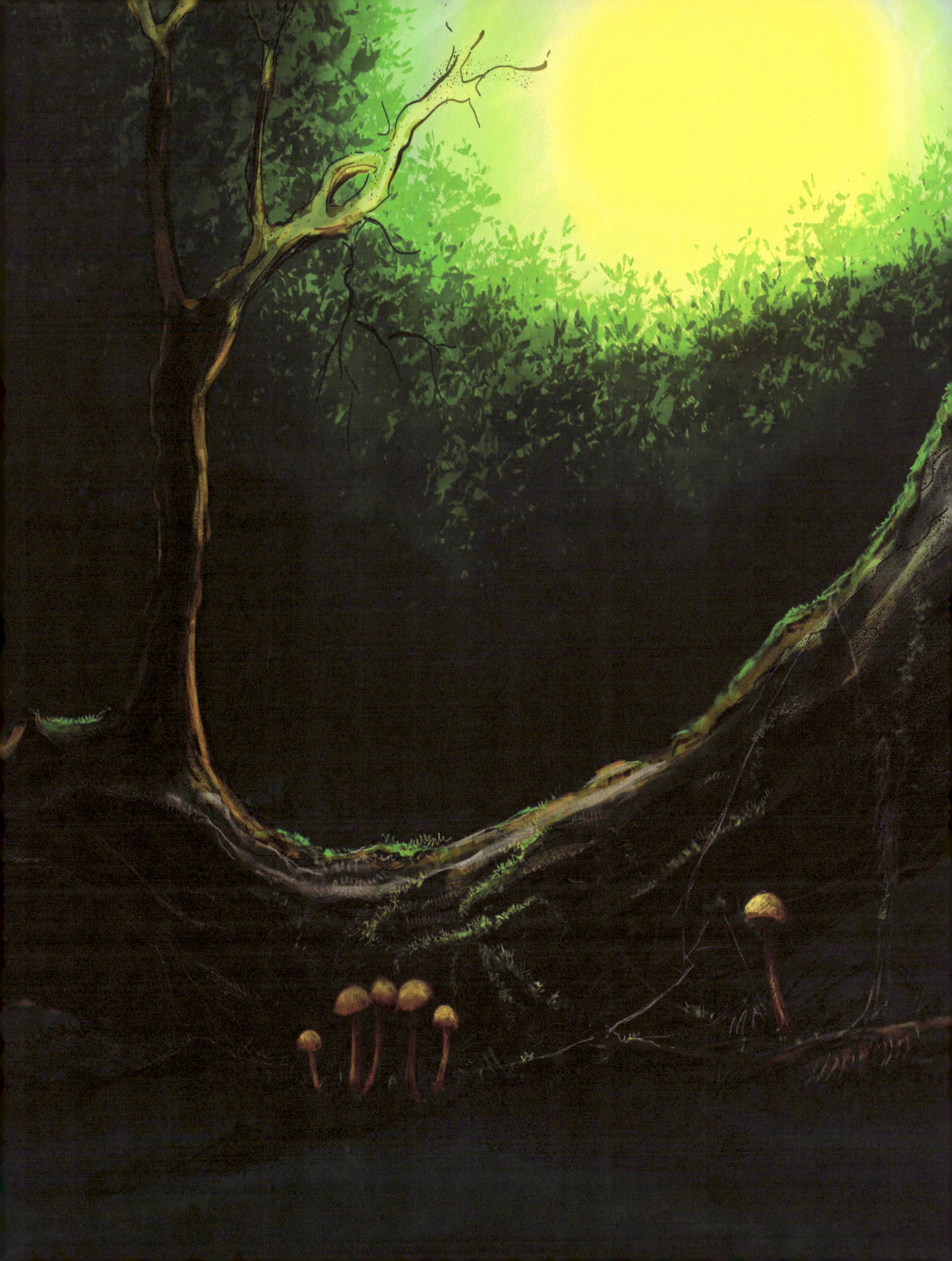

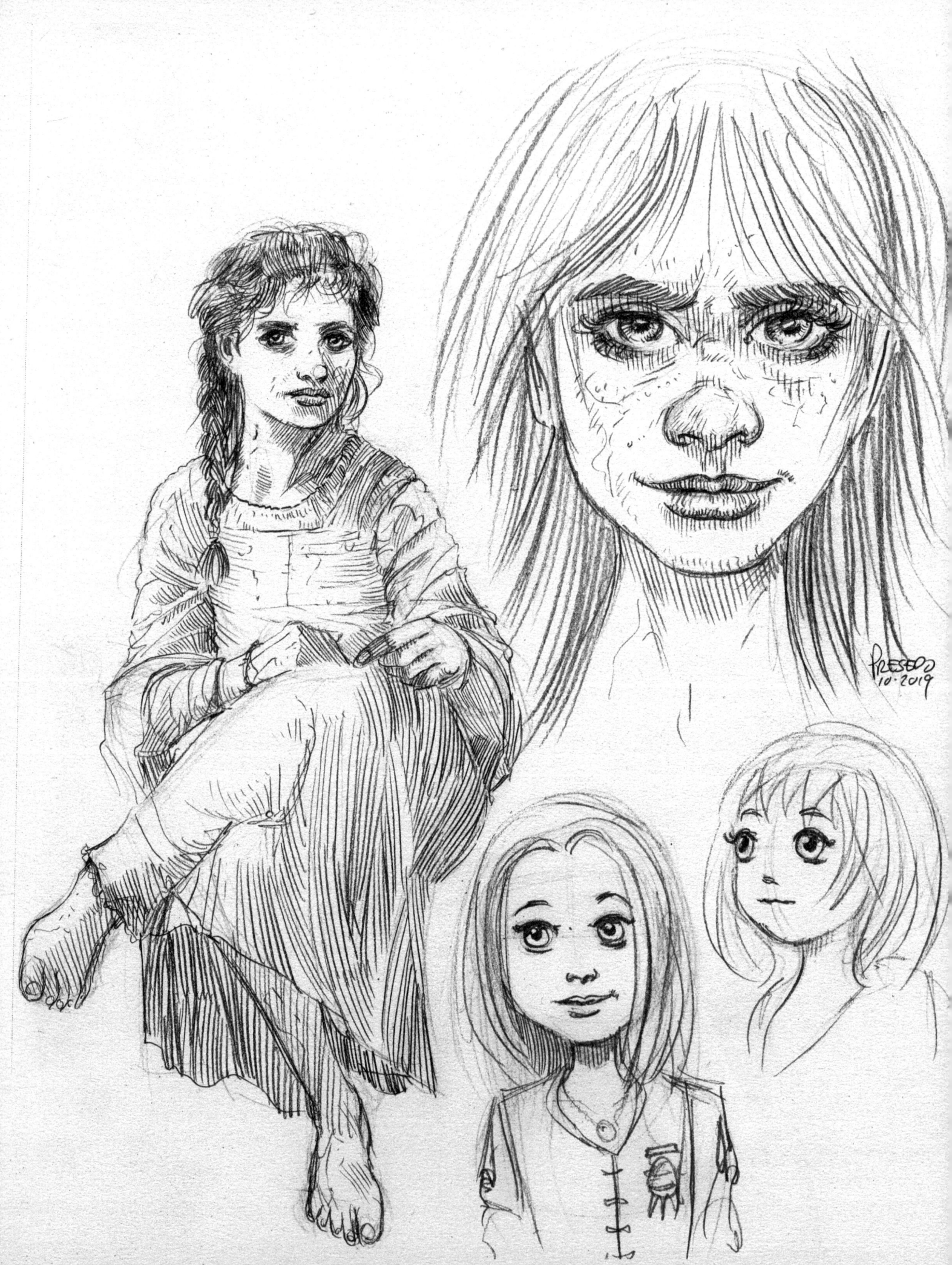

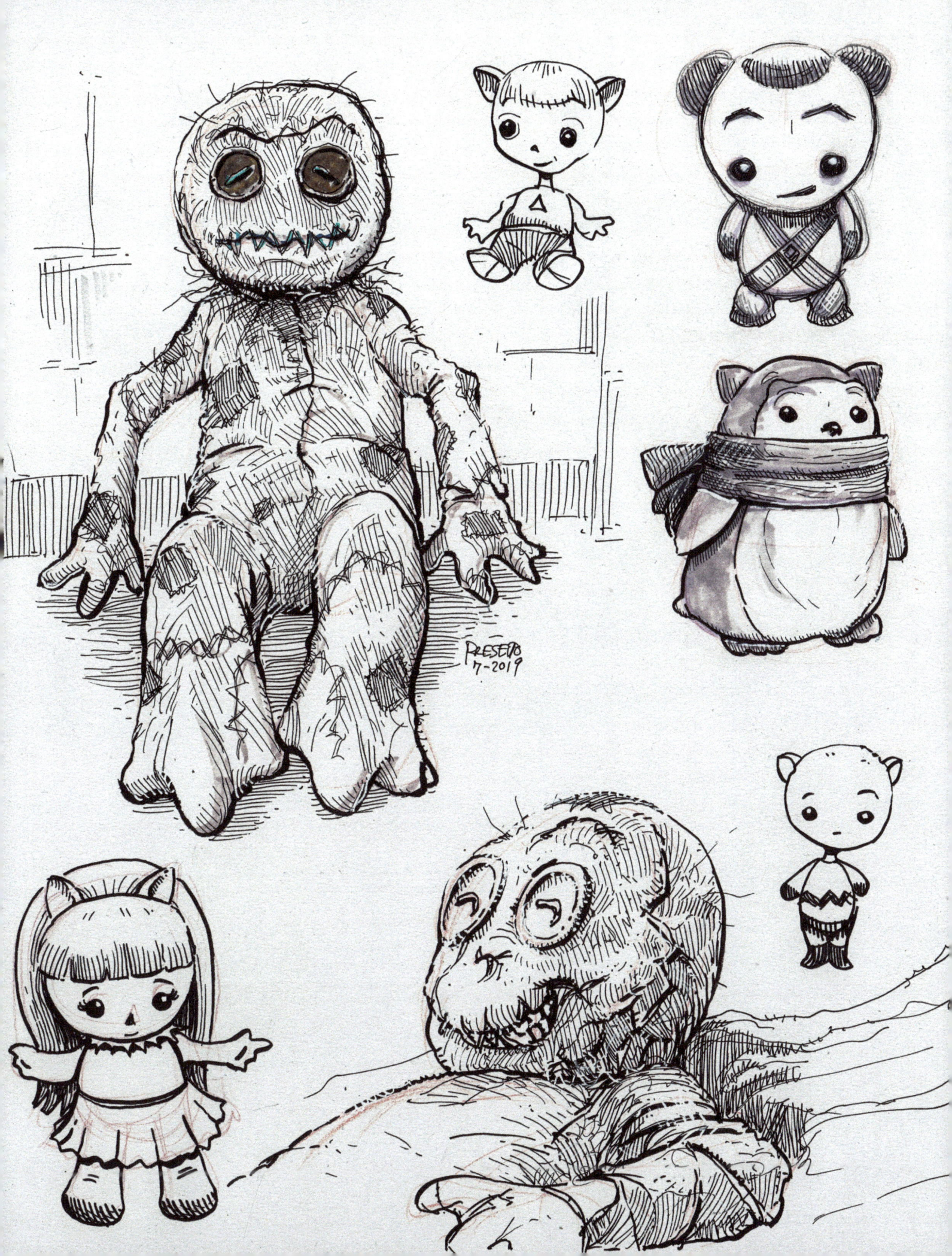

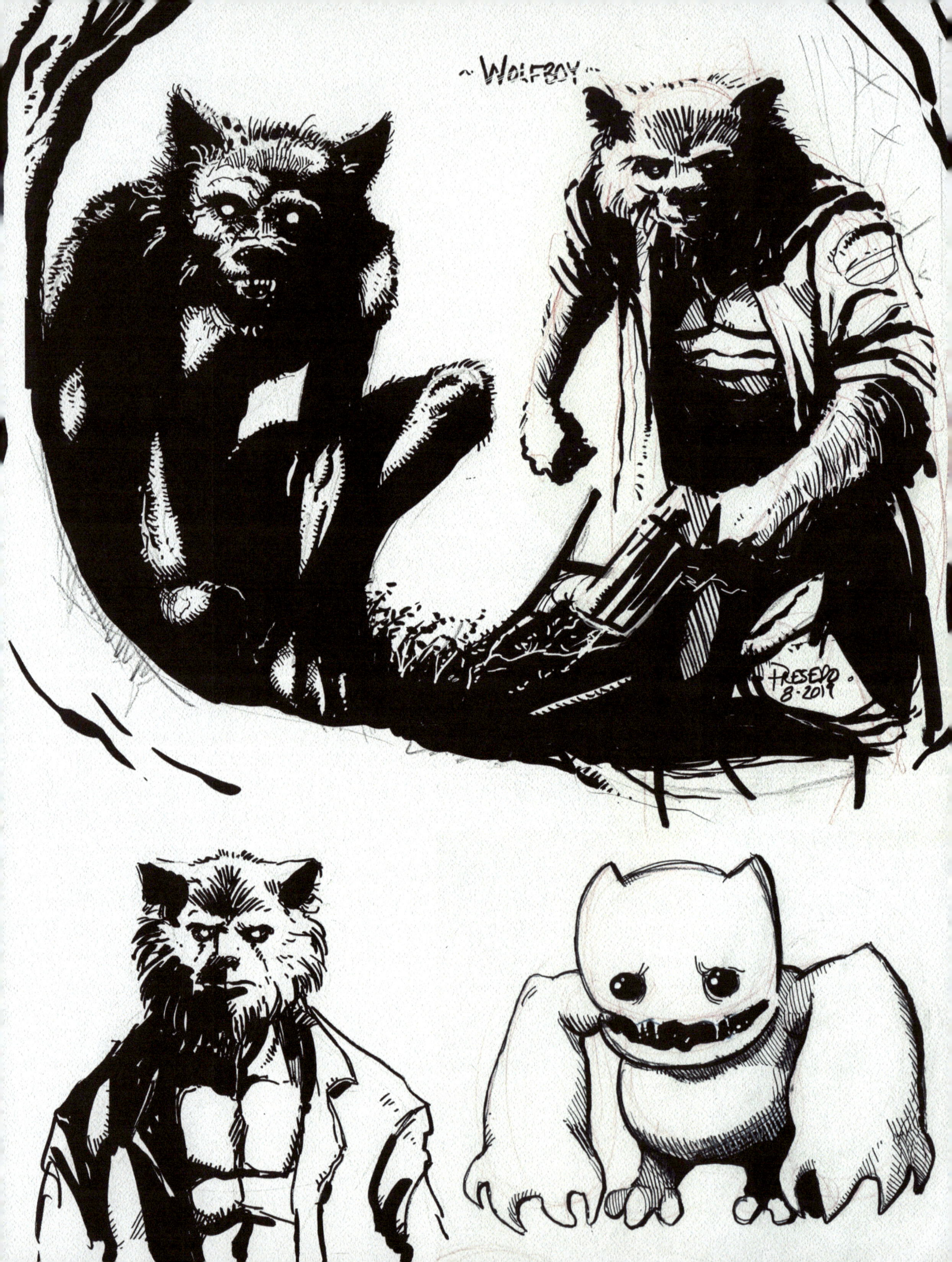

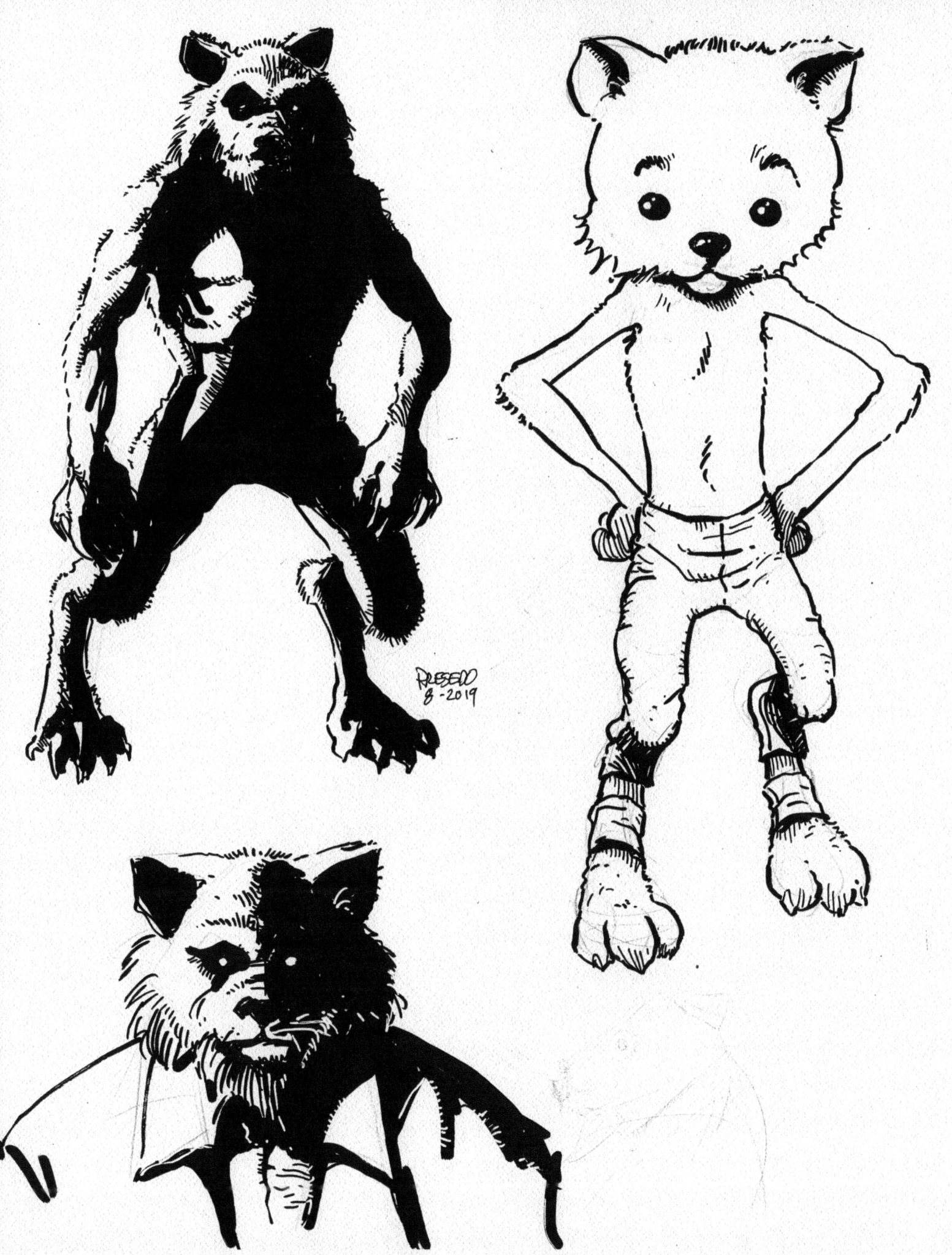

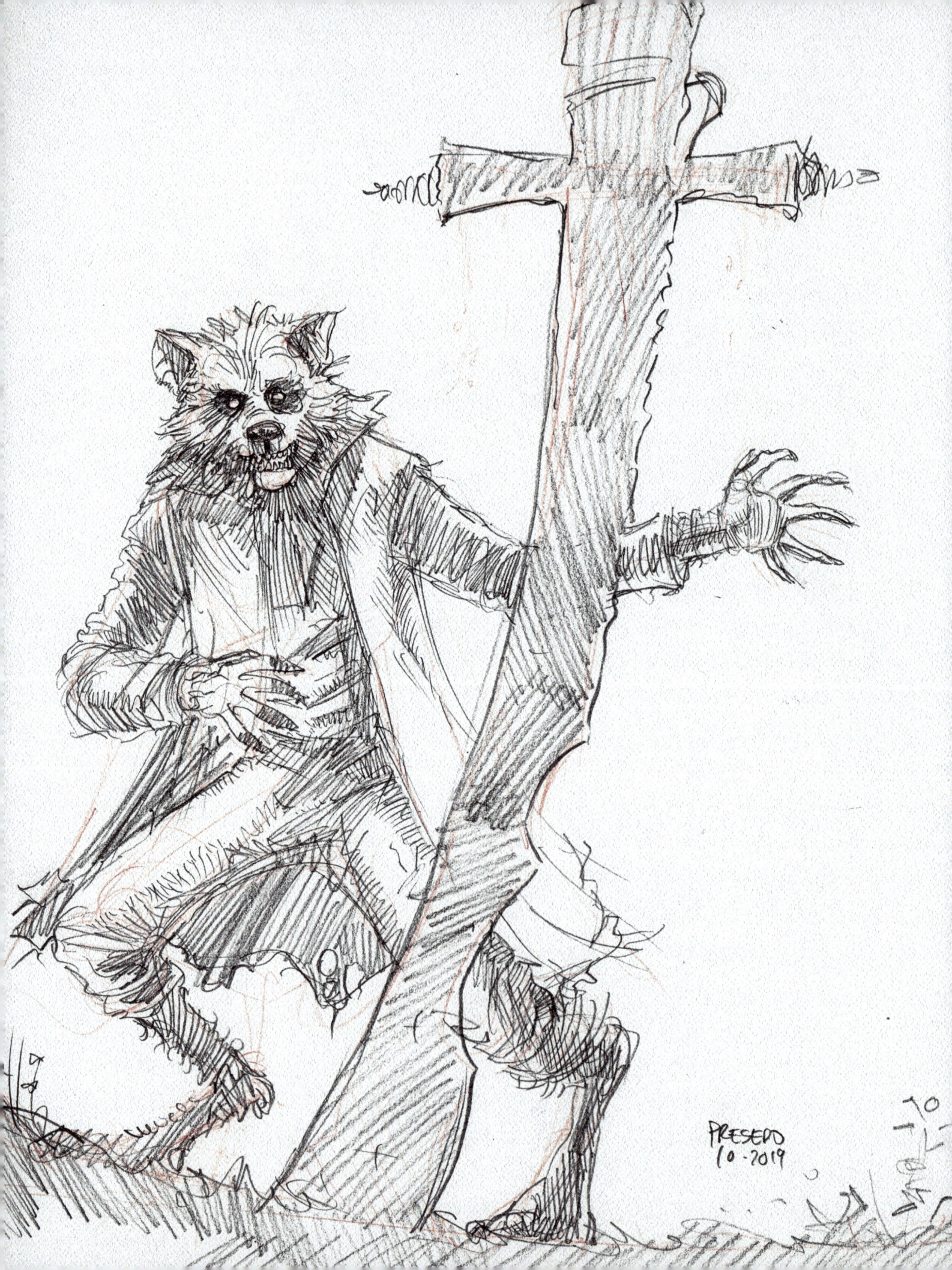

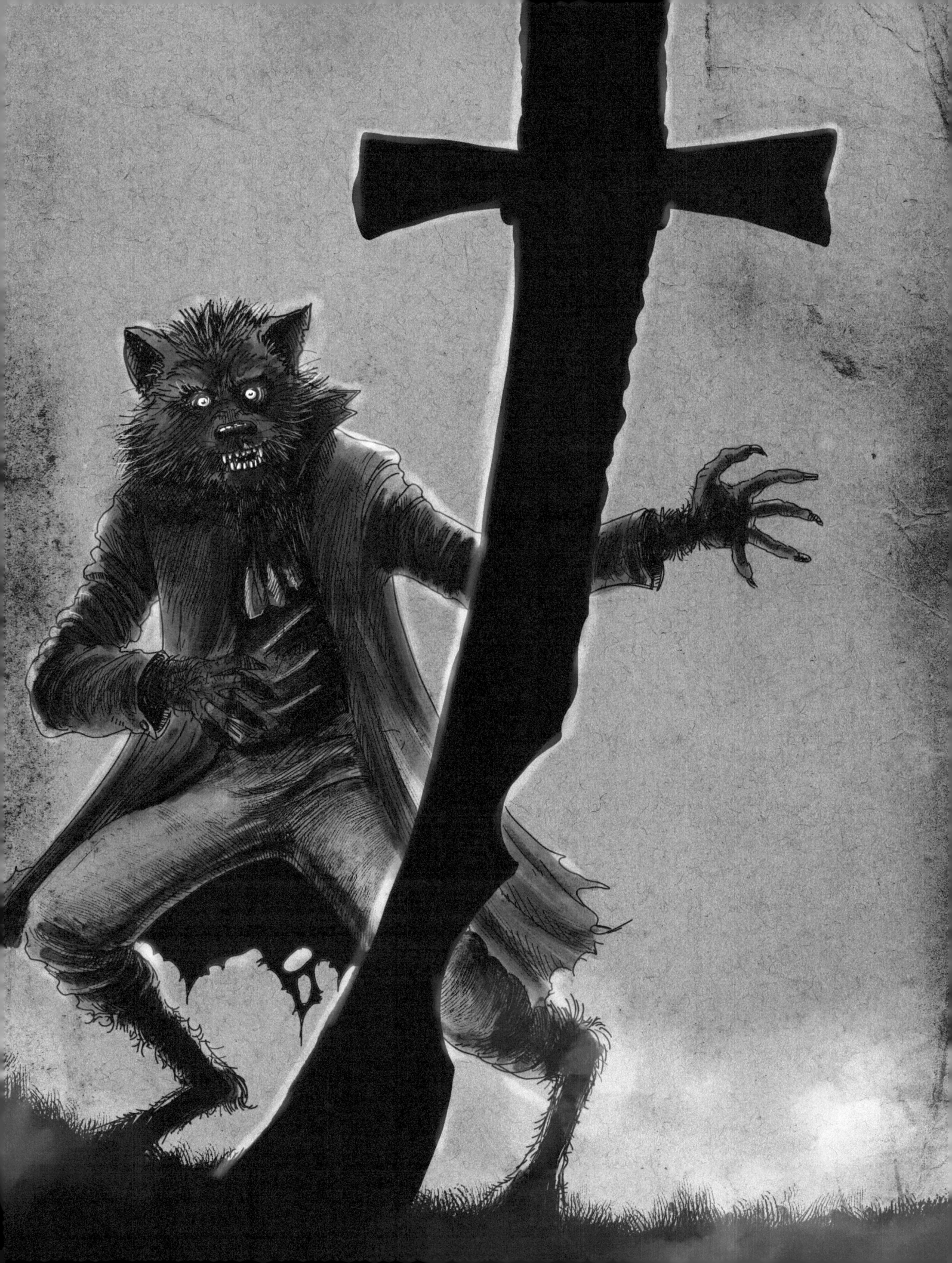

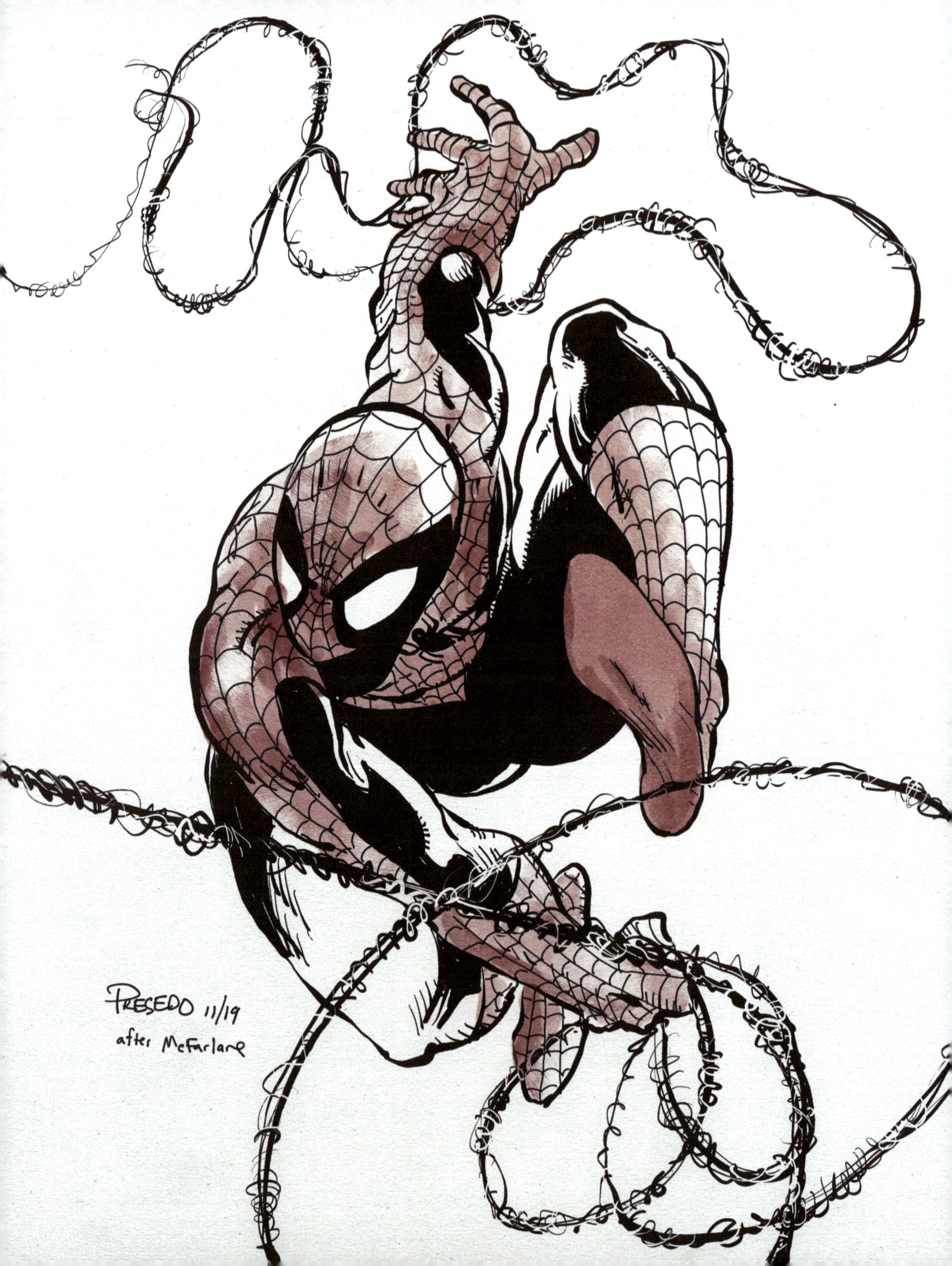

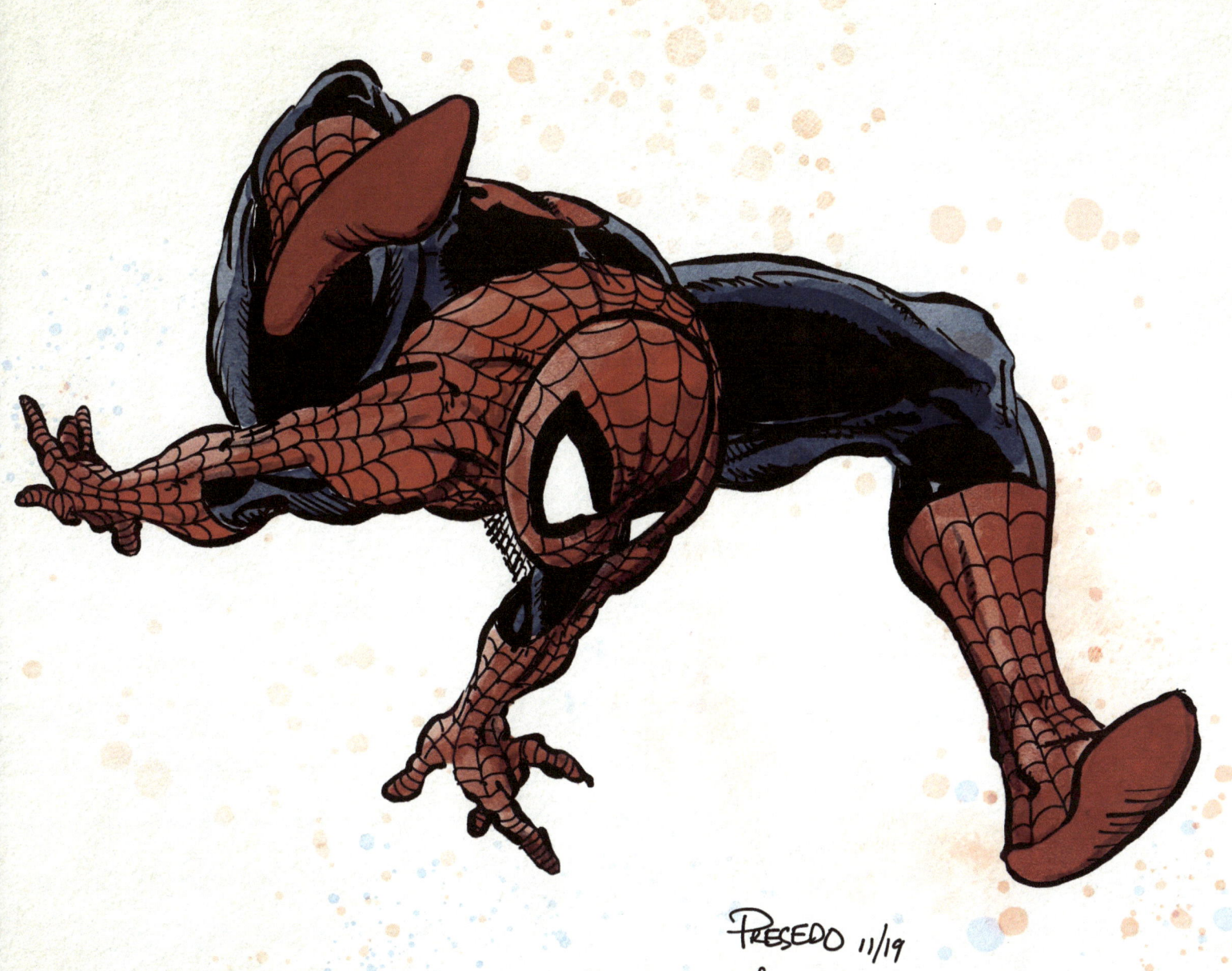

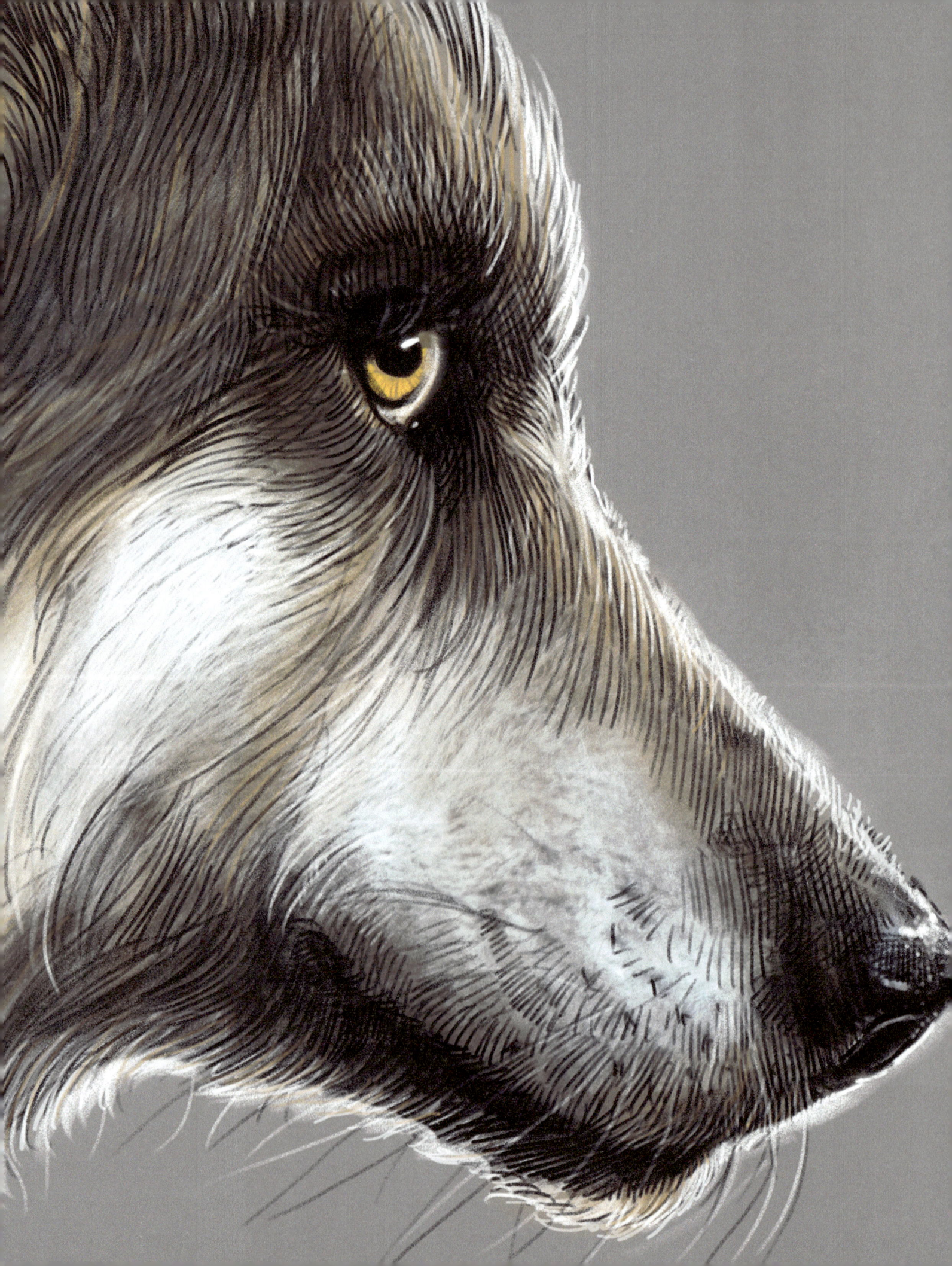

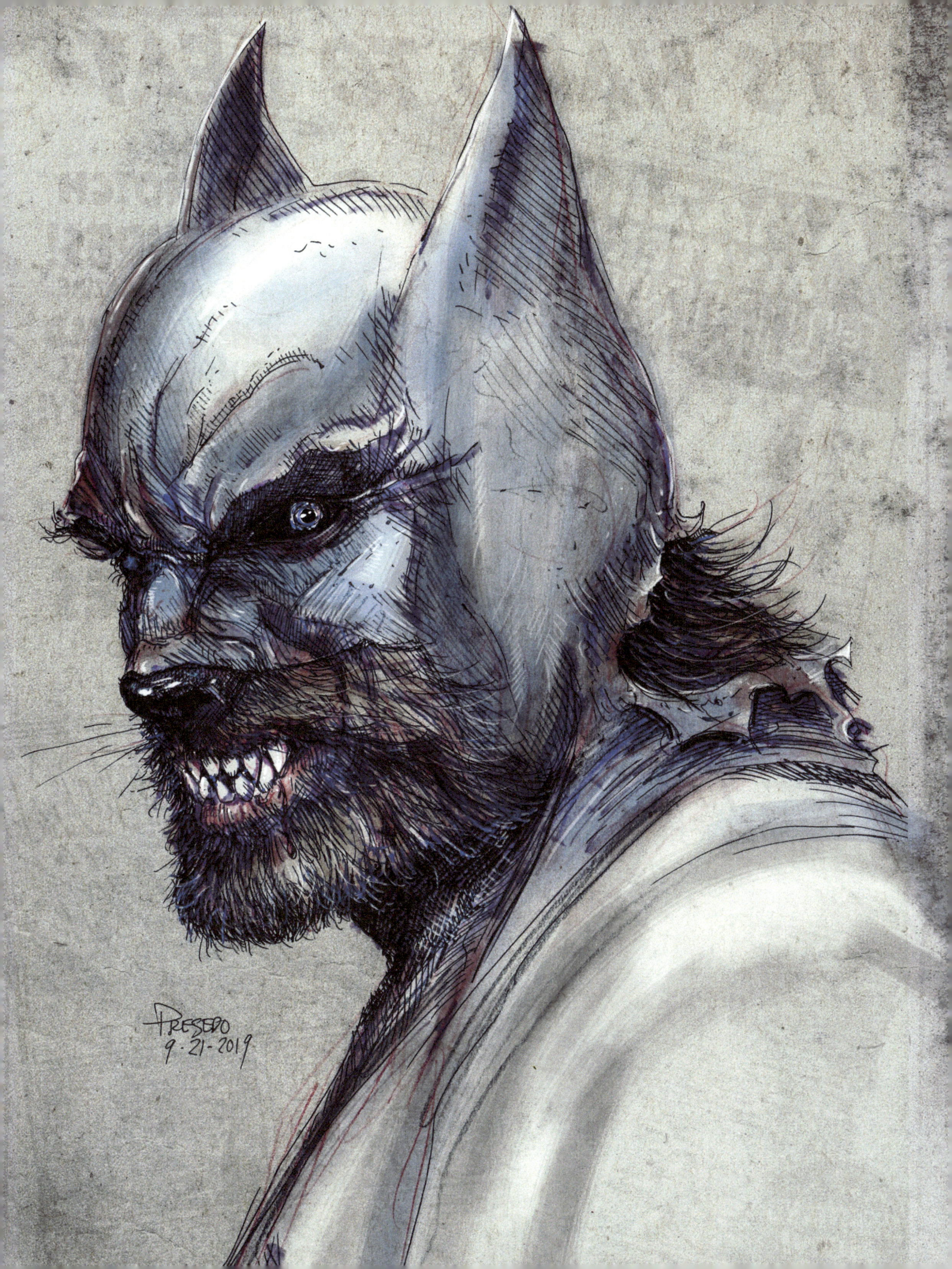

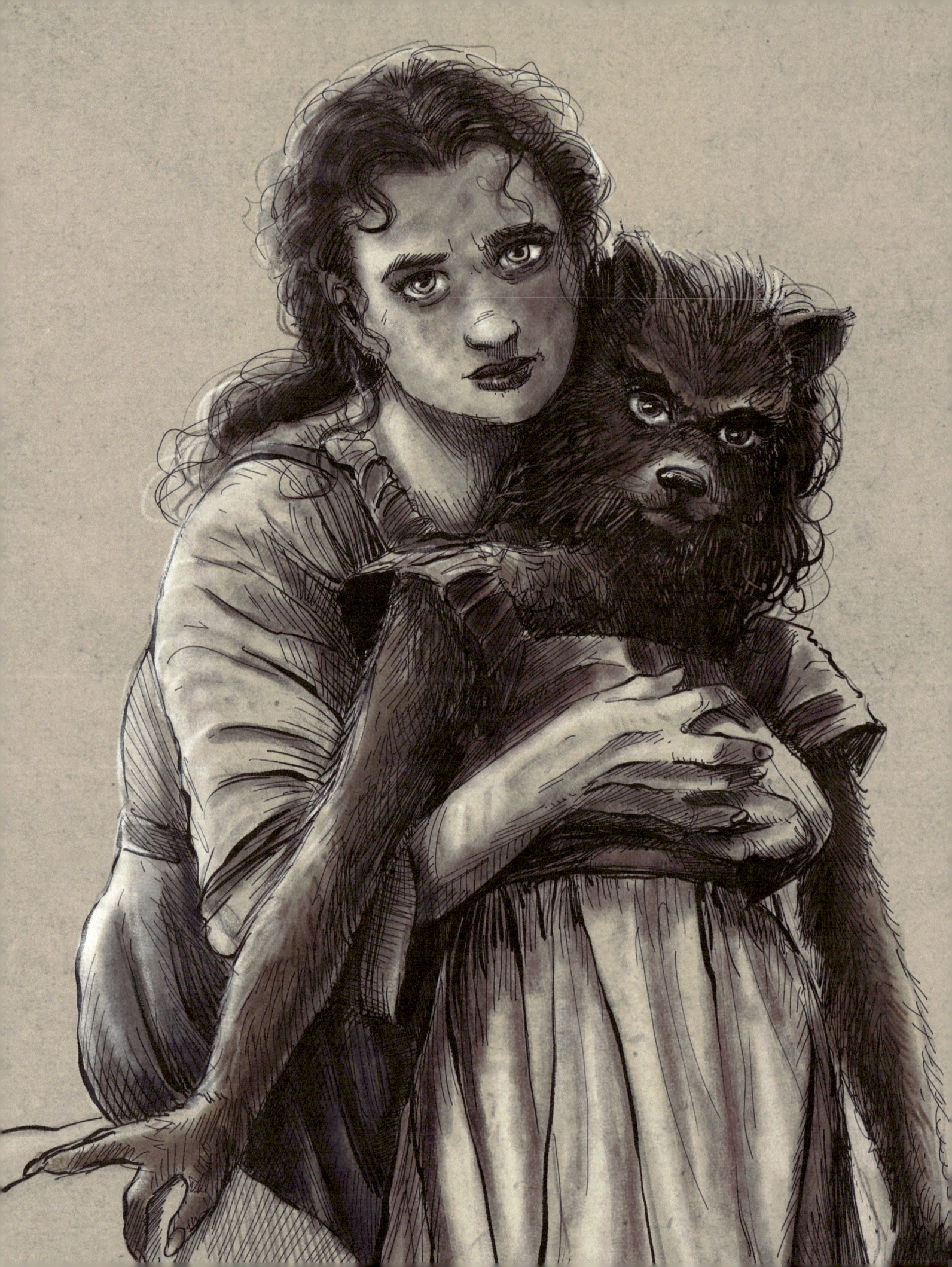

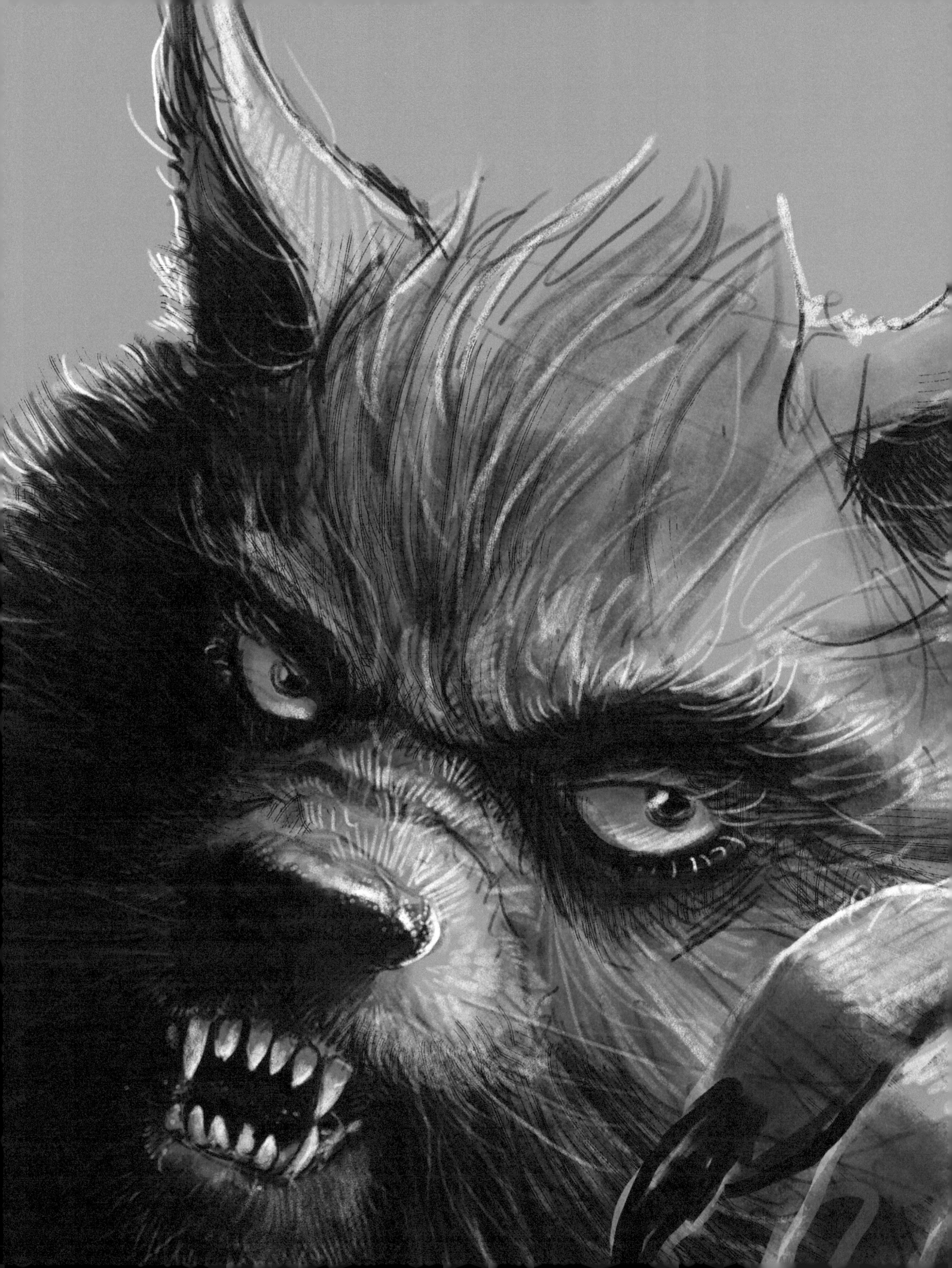

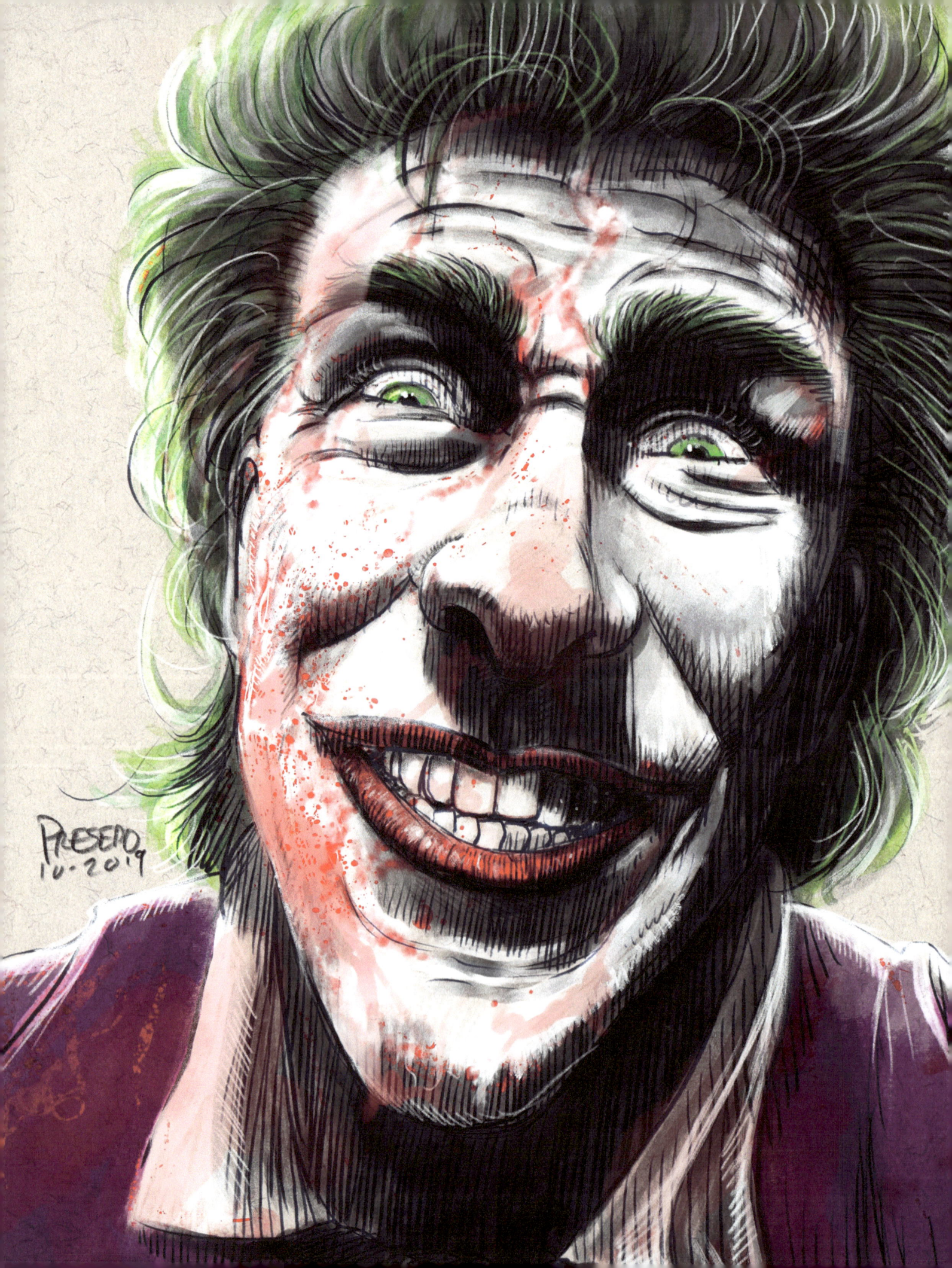

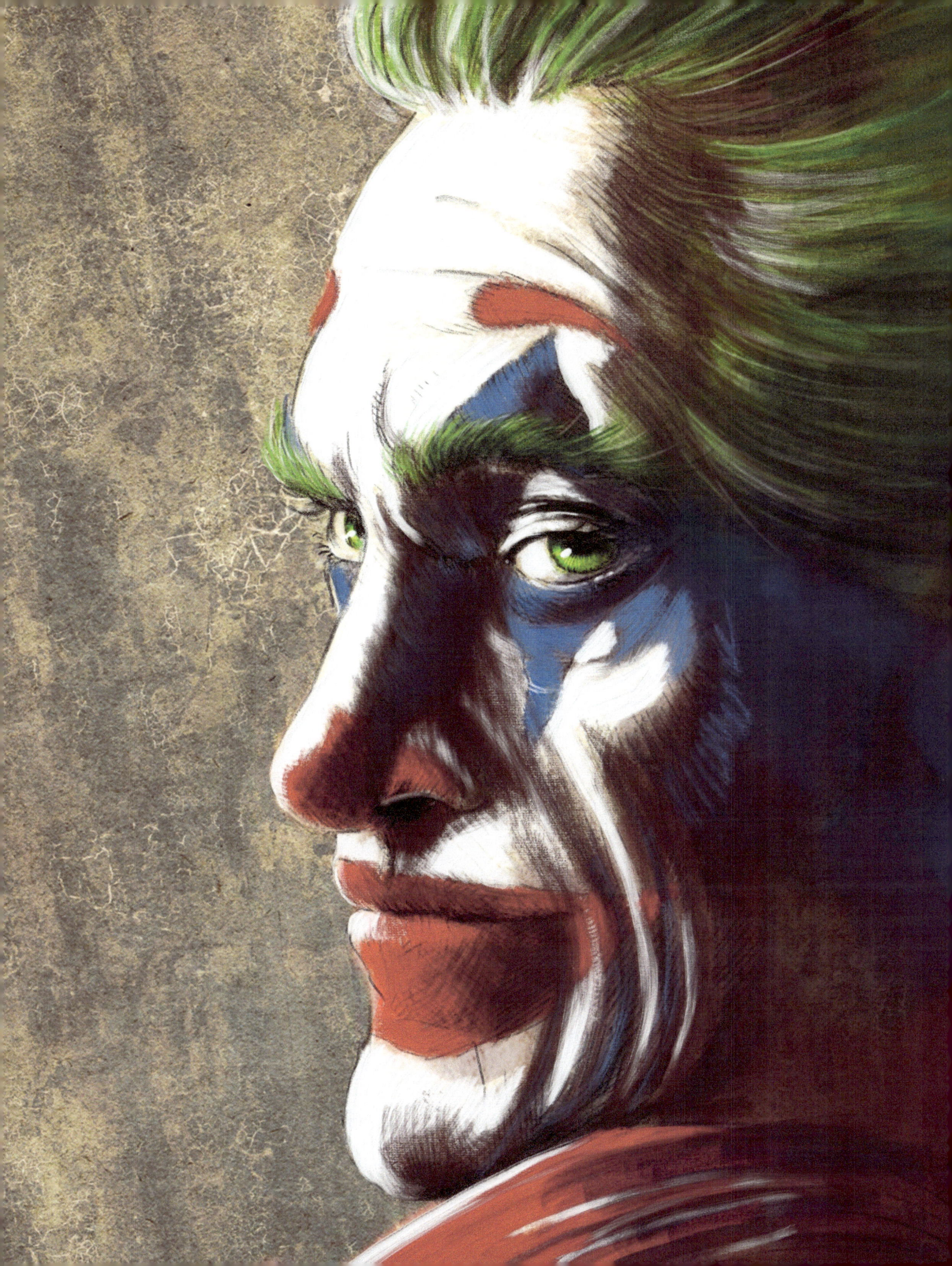

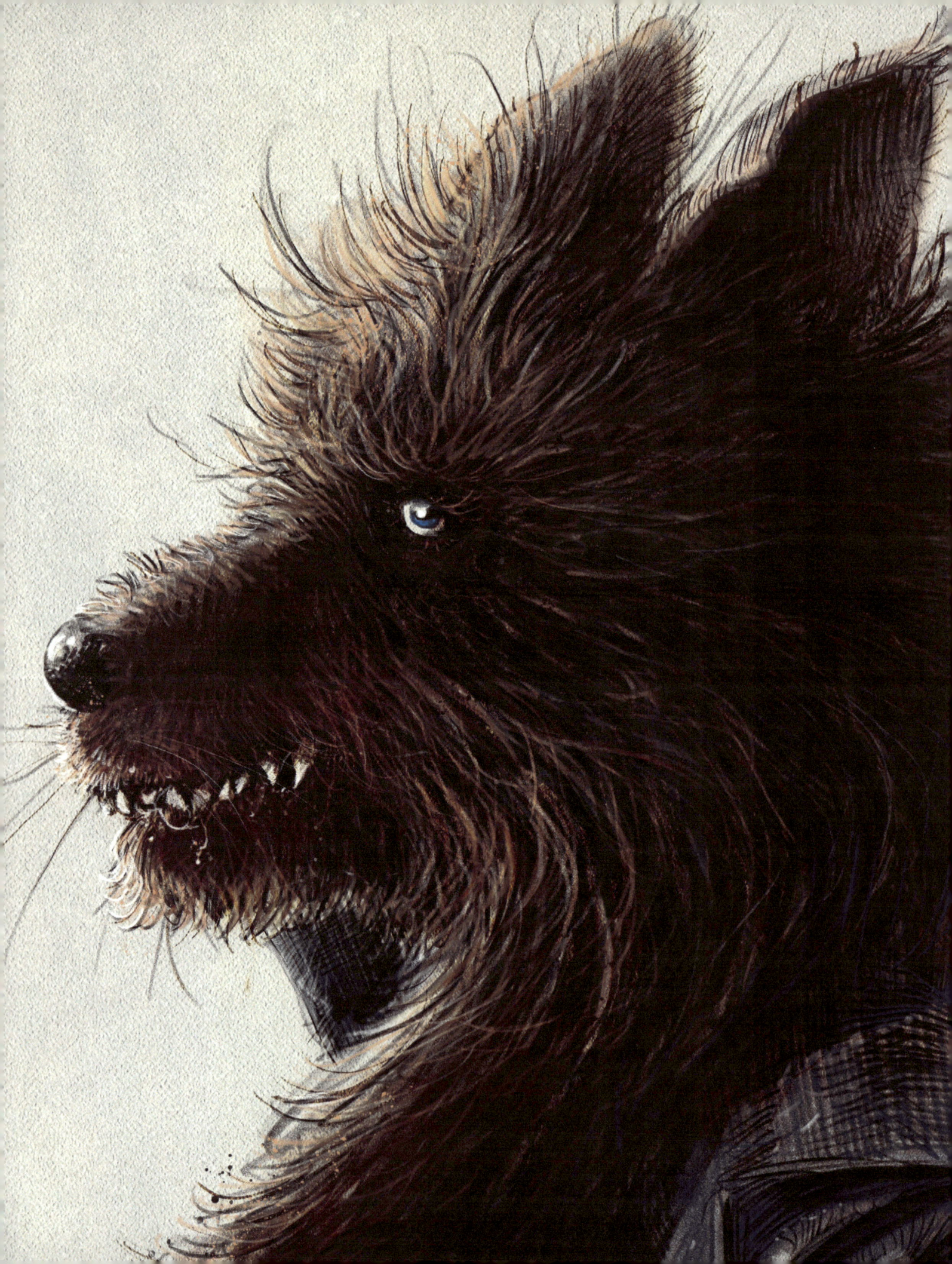

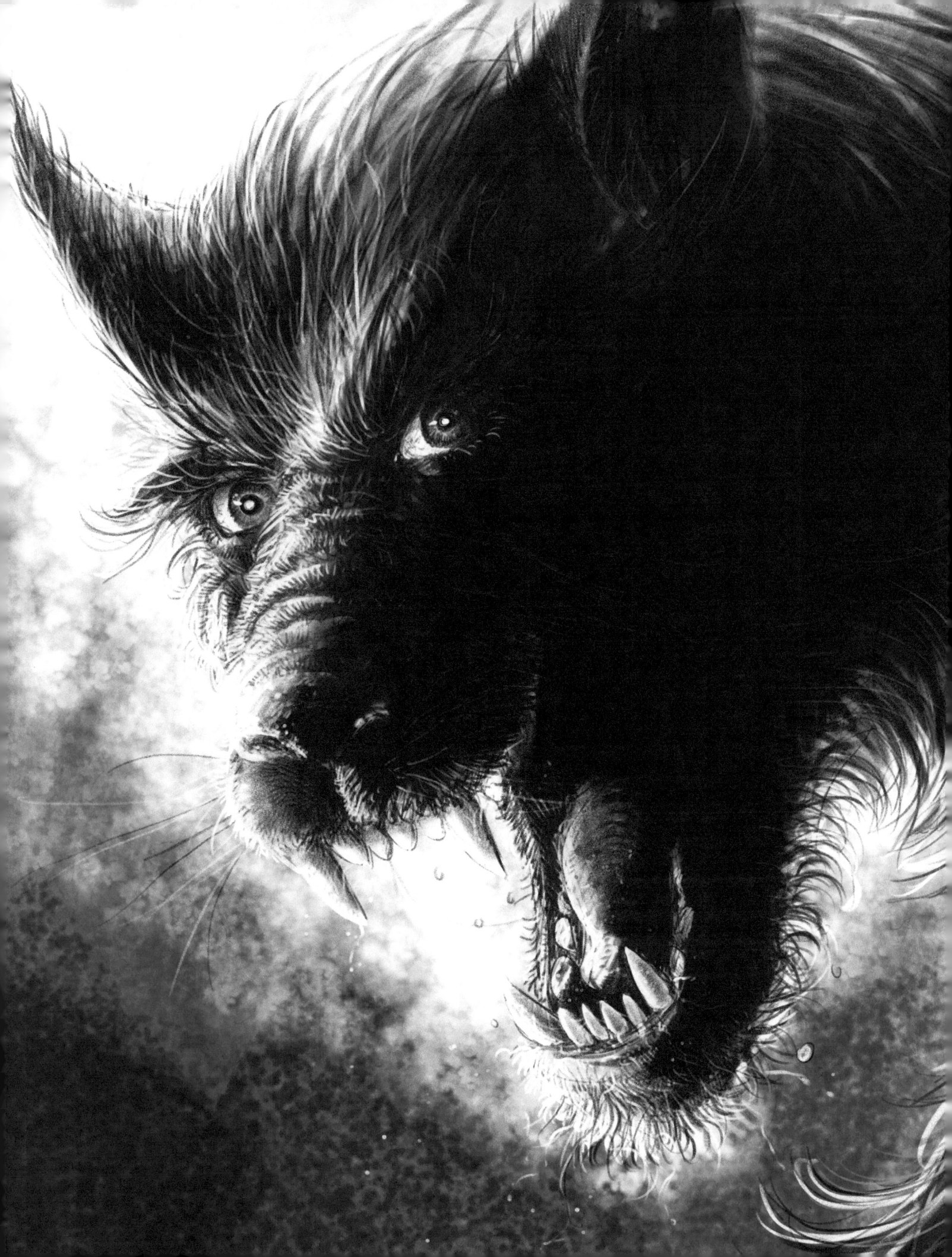

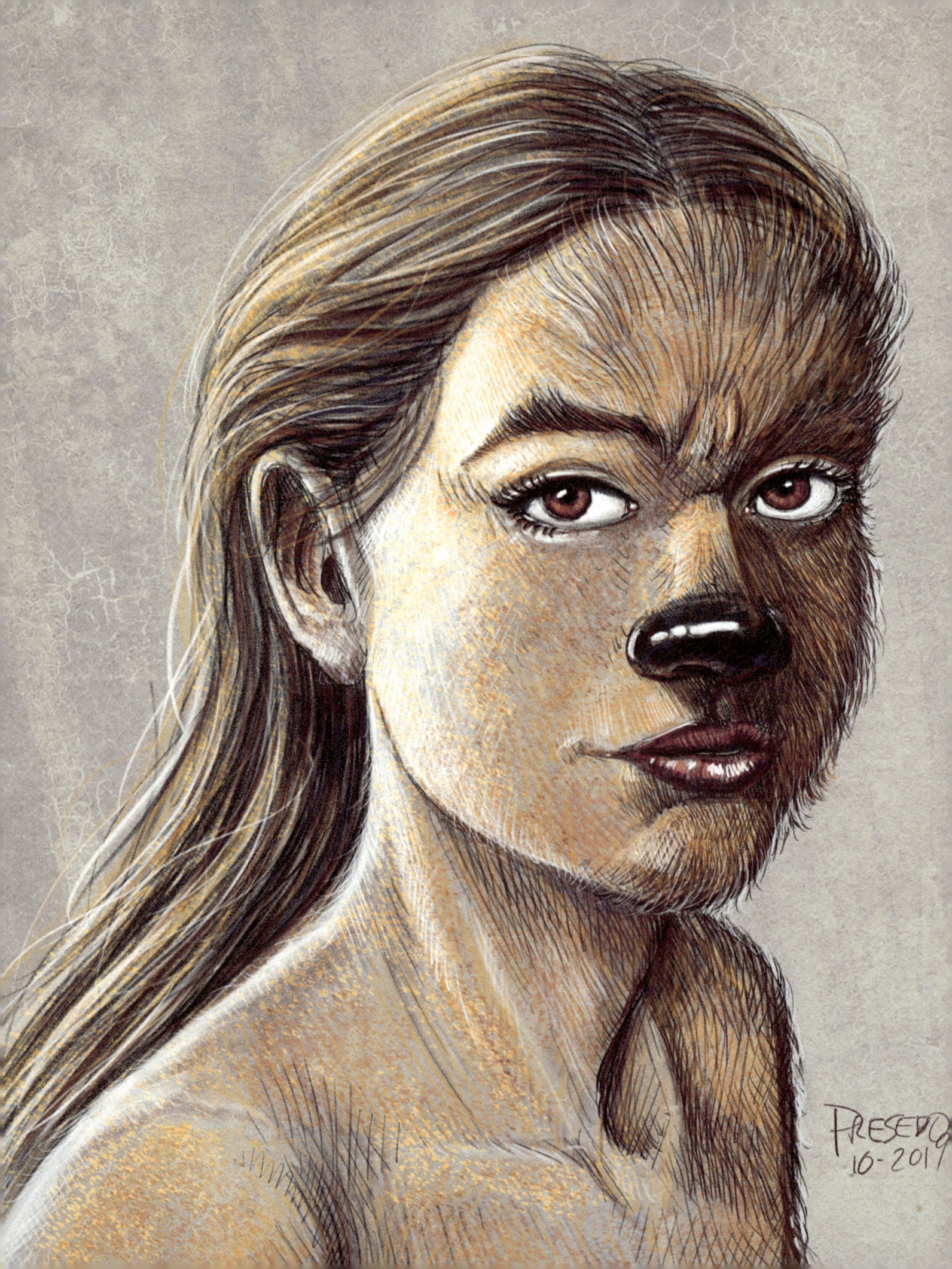

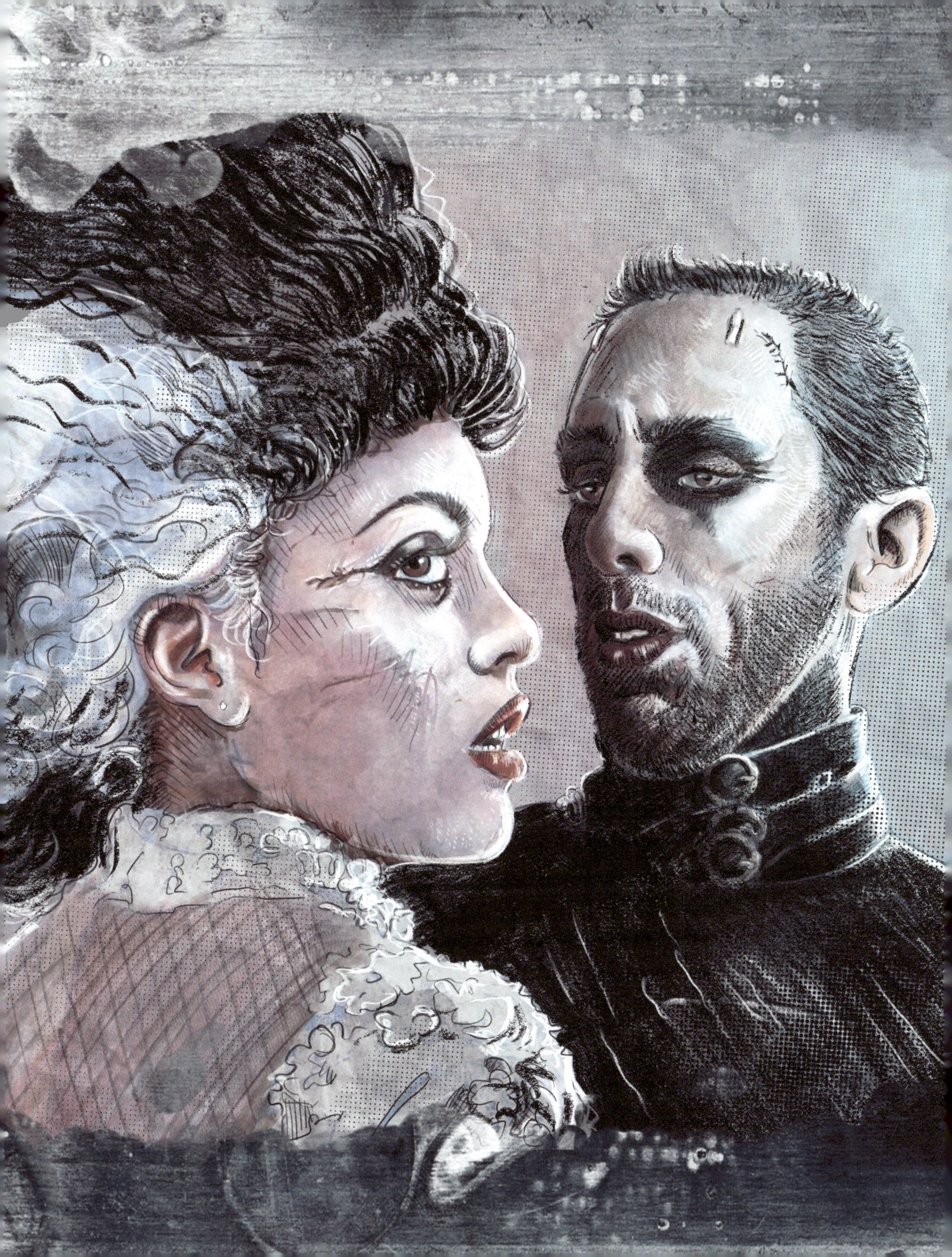

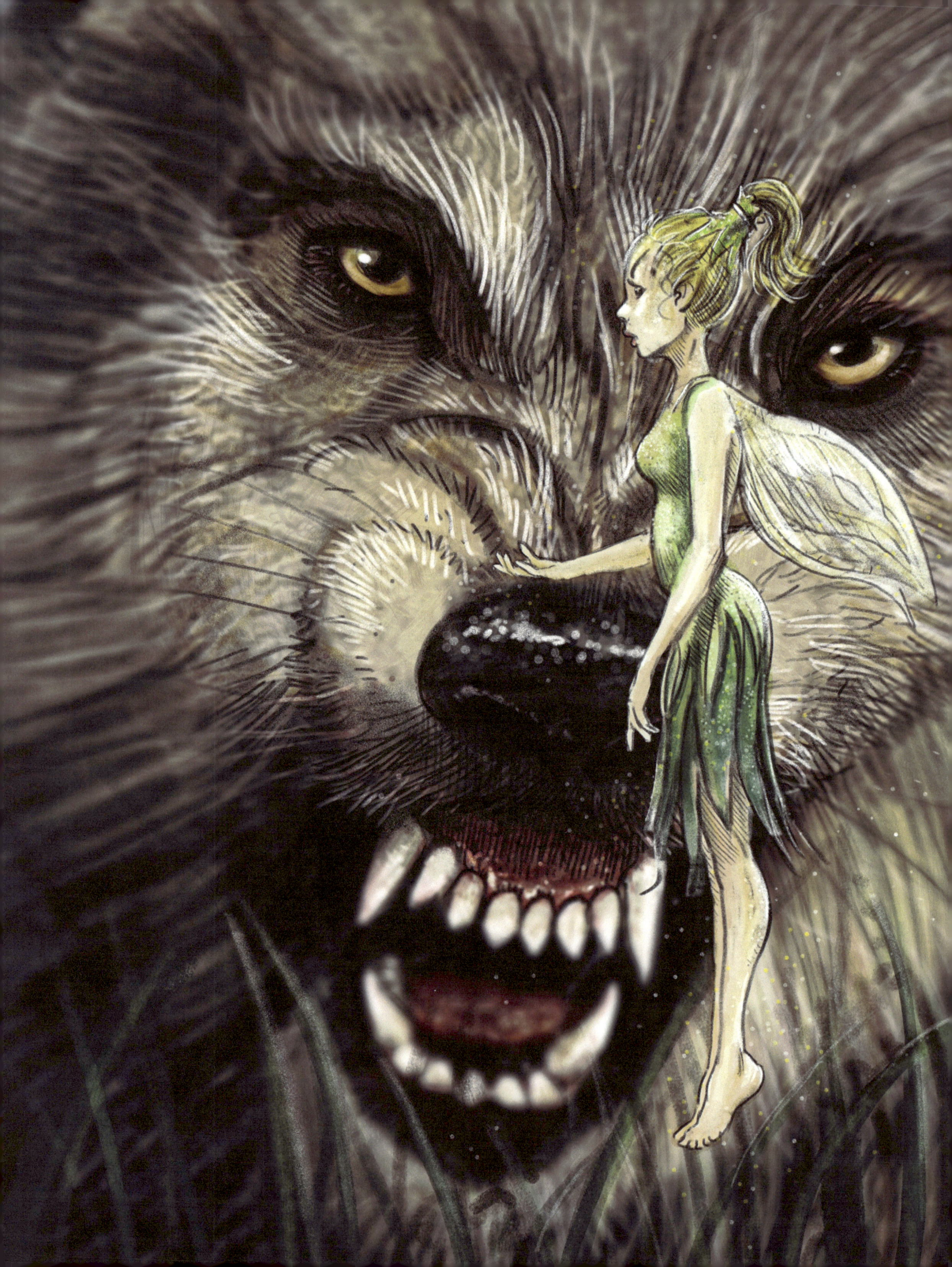

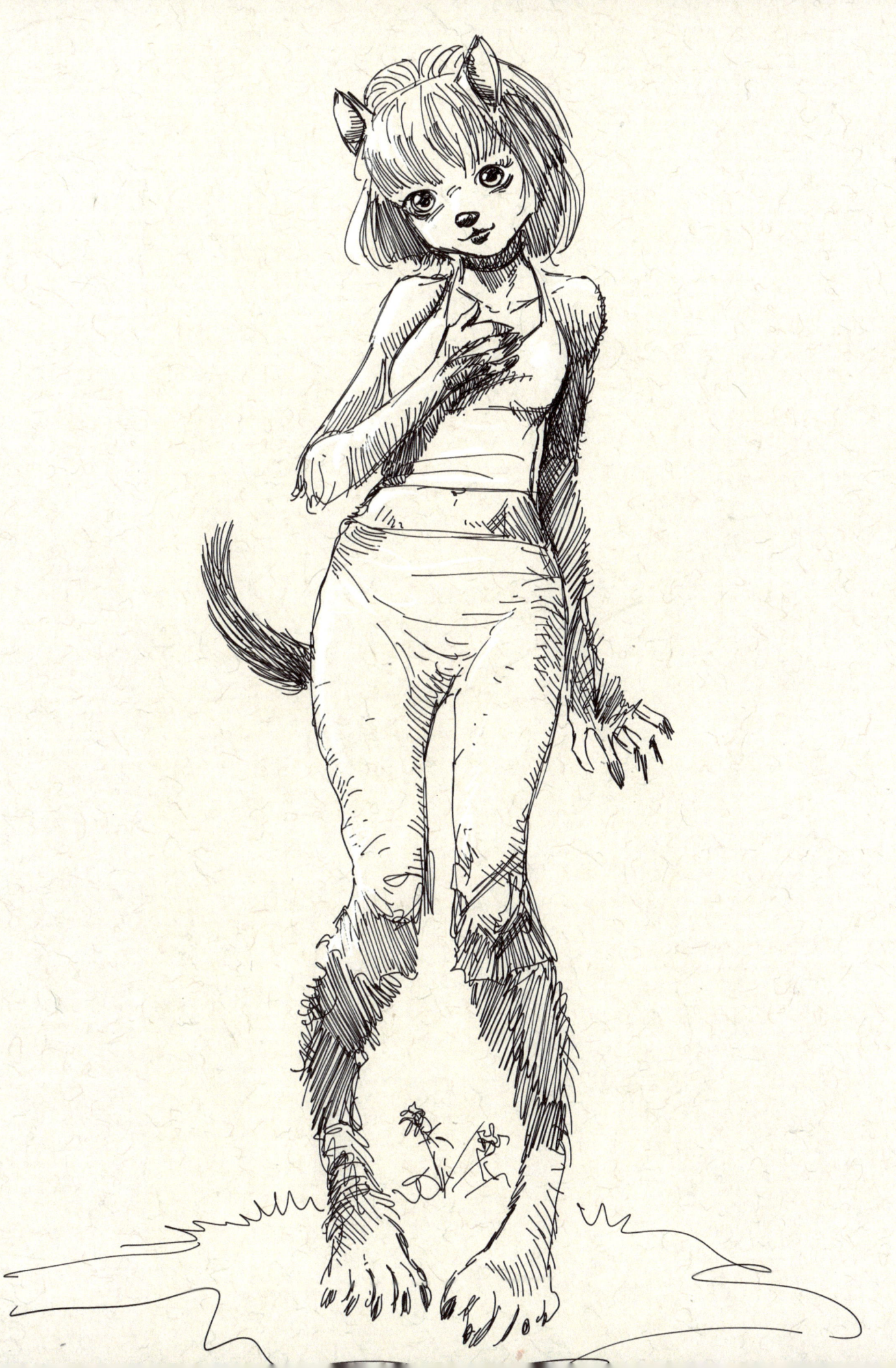

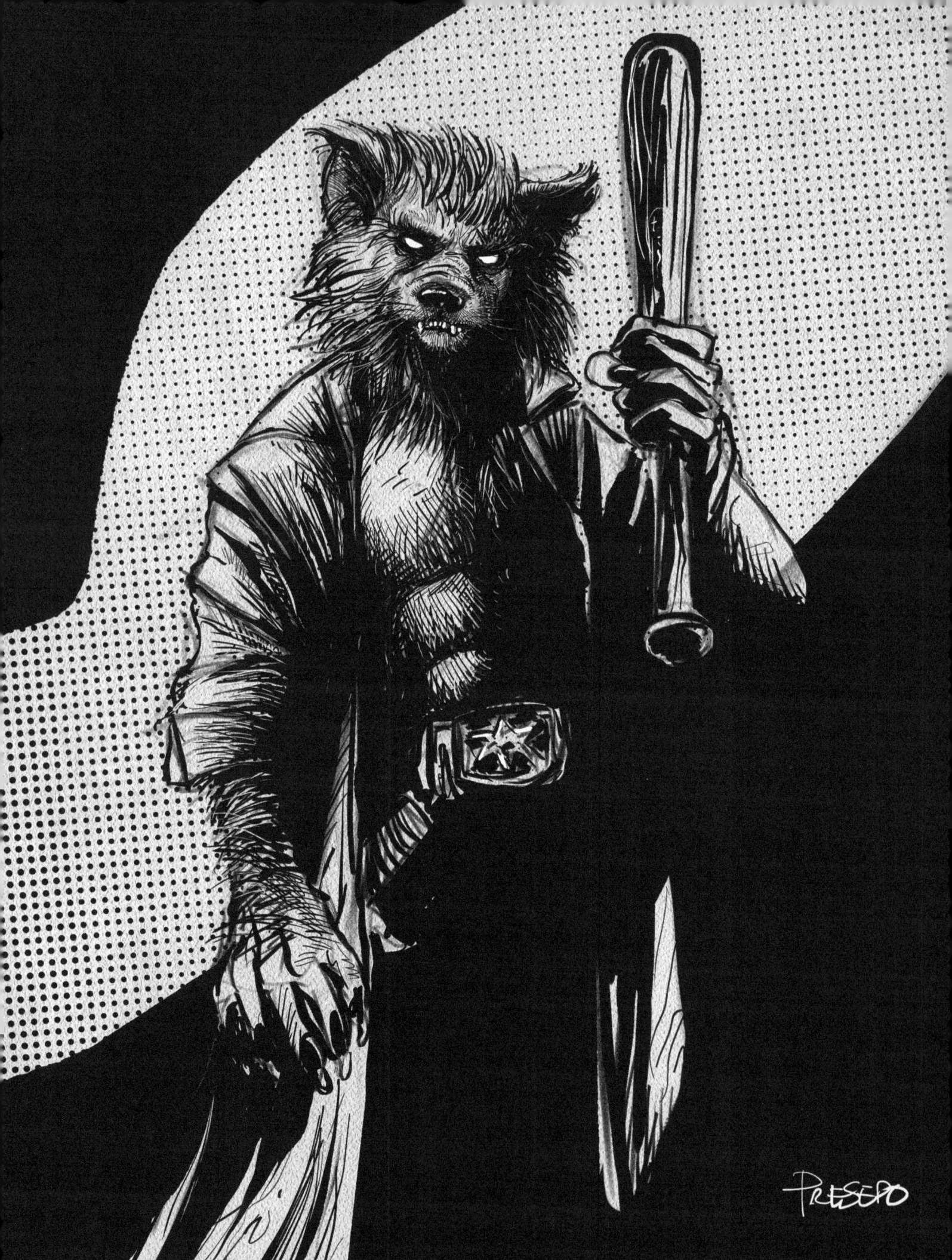

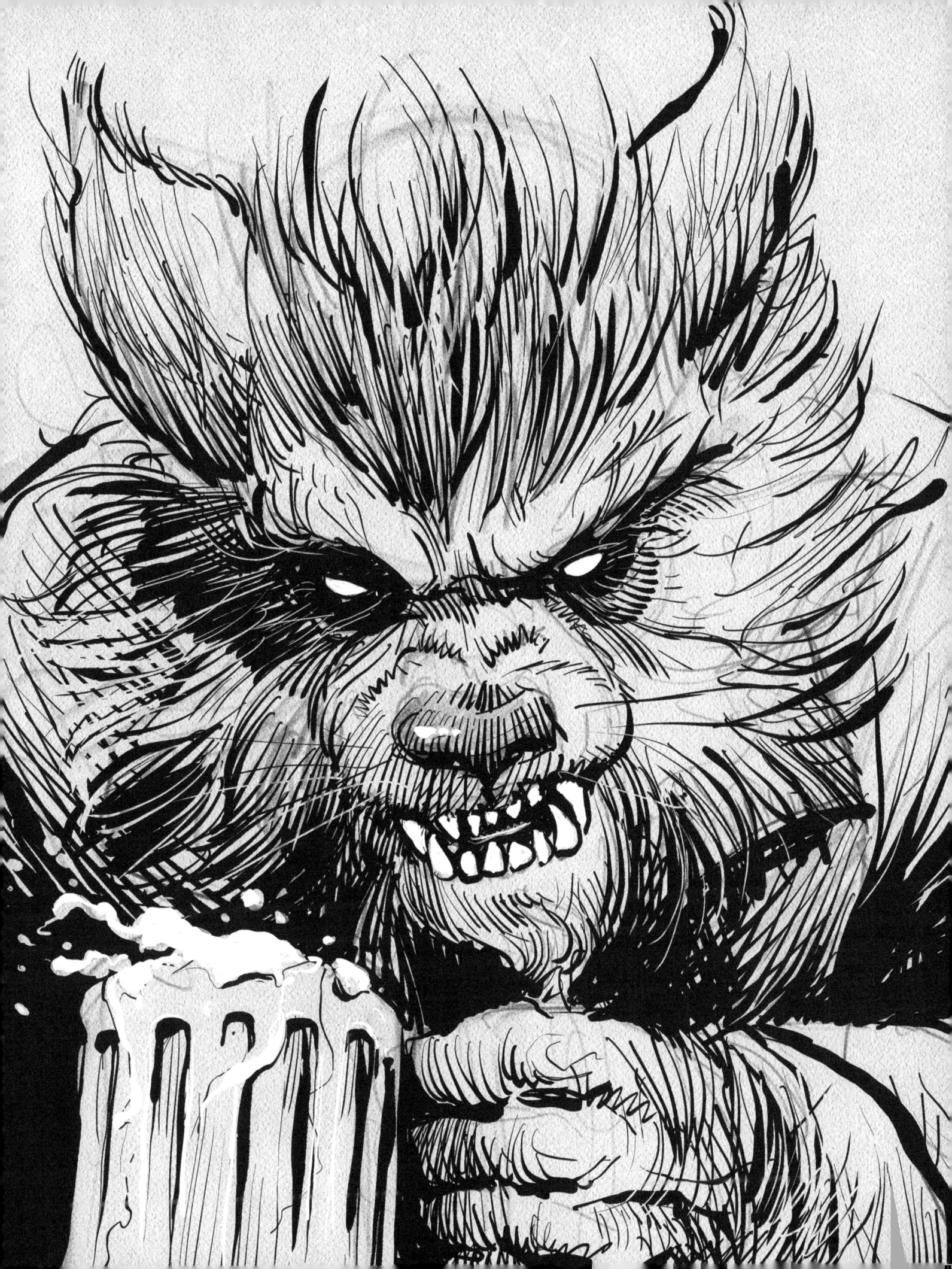

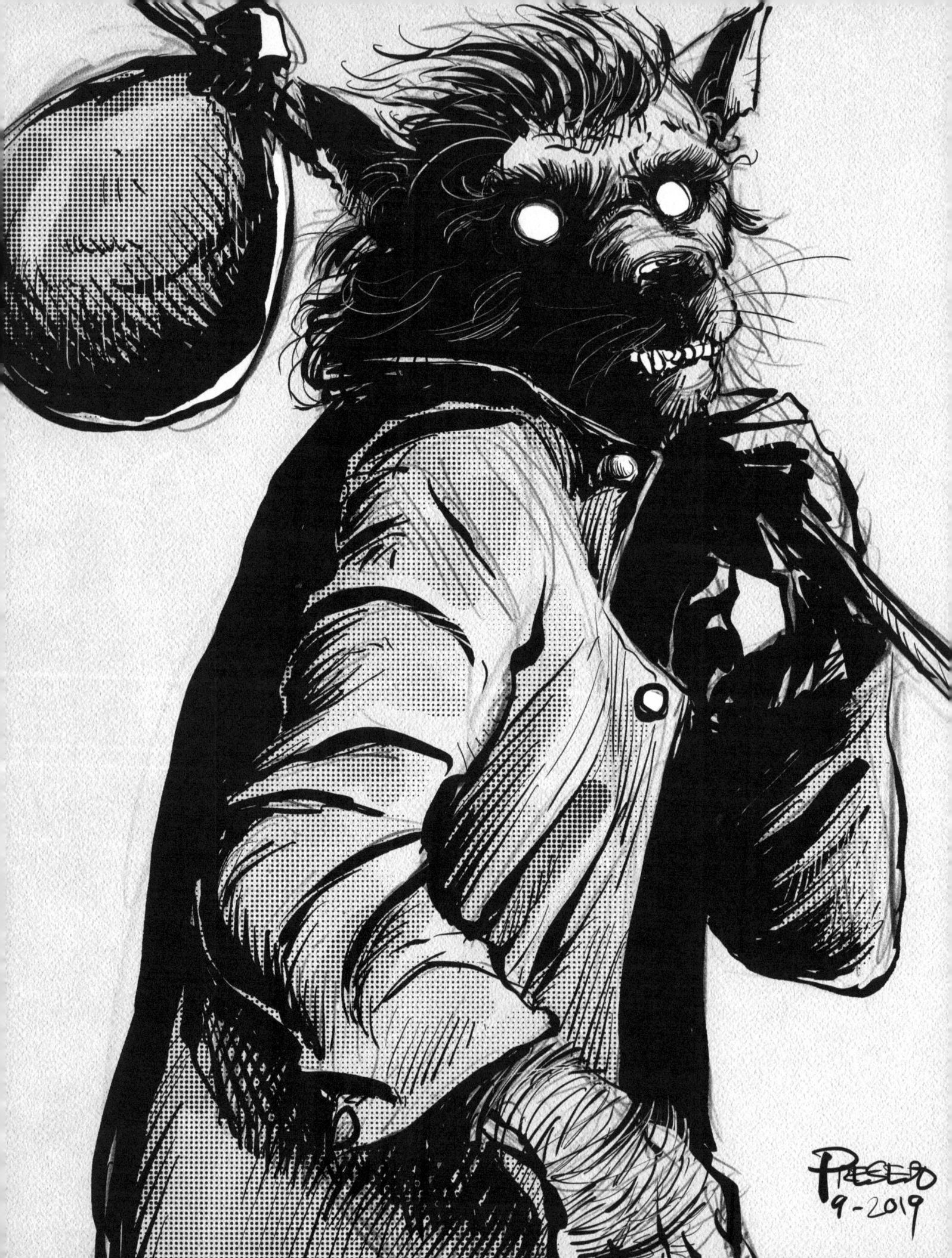

www.ingramcontent.com/pod-product-compliance
Lightning Source LLC
Chambersburg PA
CBHW040407220526
45473CB00004B/1158